Badass Ways to End Anxiety & Stop Panic Attacks!

"A counterintuitive approach to recover and regain control of your life."

Die-Hard and Science-Based Techniques to Recover from Anxiety and Stop Panic Attacks

Geert Verschaeve
Founder of ilovepanicattacks.com

TABLE OF COOLNESS

Acknowledgements

I want to thank the many founders of a different way of dealing with anxiety and panic attacks: Marcus Aurelius, Viktor Frankl, Claire Weekes, Nelson Mandela, Aaron T. Beck, Albert Ellis, and Daniel Goleman. These men and women all laid the groundwork for an innovative way of thinking centuries and decades ago.

Furthermore, I want to thank each and every one of my clients who have followed my audio course over the years. Your testimonials, feedback, wisdom, and words of thanks have made helping as many people as I can my life's most important mission.

Thanking My Anxiety

I'd like to especially thank my panic attacks and a subtle emotion called debilitating anxiety for standing by me for fourteen years.

You, the anxiety and panic attacks, were always there for me, even when I *really* didn't need you to be. Even when I would have rather flossed the teeth of a great white shark than deal with the symptoms you gave me, you were present—day in, day out—always available to pay me a visit. It seemed so effortless to you.

It had been a long time since I felt like myself, thanks to you. There's a saying, "Everything you want is on the other side of fear." The problem was I didn't know how to get to that other side because you were blocking my view.

I used to be embarrassed and ashamed. I felt weak and didn't want to be seen with you in my presence. I was afraid what other people would think of me if they noticed you hung out with me so often.

Yet, you have made me the man I am today.

If it weren't for you—and especially breaking up with you—I would have little emotional intelligence. It's thanks to you that I've learned to choose how I feel, to choose how to deal with the obstacles life throws at me. That has made life and *fully* experiencing it so much easier.

I'm now stronger than the old version of me, before the anxiety and panic attacks started.

You've also made me enjoy the little things in life—things other people take for granted. There were so many activities I disliked or totally avoided at the time that you still chaperoned me.

When I drive my car now, go to the supermarket, sit in an airplane, wait in line, travel to far-away places, talk to other people, walk into a crowded space, sit in a meeting, give a presentation, eat a meal in a group setting, or do any of the other things that previously scared me, I do so with a sense of gratitude and happiness that gives me a big smile each and every time.

I now feel at home, wherever I am and I've learned to trust my body. I now get to actually enjoy all of the experiences life has to offer, thanks to you, panic attacks and anxiety.

And now I'm looking at you, my dear reader.

Overcoming my panic attacks in 2004 has allowed me to help tens of thousands of people ever since, through my website ilovepanicattacks.com, the newsletter, the audio course, my first book, and everywhere else I try to help.

It's hard to explain but even after more than a decade of helping people, I still get a lot of satisfaction when someone transforms their life by successfully using my tips and techniques.

I don't say this to boast. I'm not special! I say this so you, the reader, know that what follows shouldn't be taken lightly. It has already helped a lot of people.

I will step on your toes, undoubtedly. I will say things that will make you believe I must have lost my mind. I can assure you, I haven't.

I've been where you are and found a way out. The way out is not always intuitive. It's not always easy. If it were, everyone would find it easily and no help would be needed.

Did what I found work for everyone? No. It didn't. I'm not an angel with miracle powers, sadly. But I wouldn't still be here, investing so much of my time in helping people and making it my life's work if I didn't see that an overwhelming majority of the people who try it are able to get better.

I've seen people transform their lives when they themselves and those who surrounded them had already given up. These people believed their anxious state and the avoidance that often accompanied it was something that would be there forever. They thought they would just have to learn to manage it all, especially since they had already tried countless therapies before. They were luckily wrong. You'll read some of their stories throughout this book.

My goal in this book is to give you that same transformation.

Please write down today's date on your calendar. This is the day that your life will start to change. You're about to learn strategies and make changes that will help you improve far beyond the anxiety issues that you bought this book for. And you'll have your panic attacks or anxiety to thank for it.

Before We Start

Without wanting to sound like a know-it-all, I think I know how you feel.

When anxiety or panic strikes for the first time, all you want to do is get out of there, wherever you got that wave of fear. When it strikes for the fifth time, you may decide it's best to avoid that particular location altogether.

But then—and this also happens when your anxiety is not linked to a location at all—you see that the anxiety tends to follow you around. There is no running; there is no hiding. It's inside of you. It's a part of you.

The day you had that realization was probably not a great day. How can you possibly avoid *that*? There's no running from our own selves. That's when you might have come to the conclusion that you'd just have to learn to live with it.

I've been there, too. Overcoming this type of anxiety seems impossibly hard.

You may also believe you're different than "normal" people. Or even that your anxieties are different compared to the ones other anxious people suffer from. You may be convinced that you're alone in this.

Please allow me to set the record straight from the get-go. **You are not alone.**

And there is a way out. Those I've helped and I are living proof of this. And again, I'm not that special. Millions of people have overcome their anxieties without any of my help.

There's just one real prerequisite.

You'll need to commit! You will need to decide right now that you've had it with your anxiety-related issues and that you'll persevere. If you do that, you'll be surprised what will follow in the next couple of weeks and months.

It won't be easy, but we're in this together.

My Story

My panic attacks started at around the age of nine. I was pretty careless before that age. I had lots of friends and no worries at all. I was only afraid of the monsters in my closet and the shark from *Jaws*, a movie I saw while I was too young. Yet at that age, I had my first real panic attack during New Year's Eve. The symptoms were so debilitating that I'll never forget the experience.

I didn't get what was happening. It was as if I couldn't control what I was feeling. That was frustrating since, at the same time, I tried to hide my symptoms from the other people present. I didn't want to ruin their night or become the center of attention. I had severe dizziness; my vision was starting to get pitch black as if I was going to faint and even lose consciousness. I had nausea, a pounding heart, and tingling sensations on my skin. Even though it was in the middle of winter, I felt like someone had decided to host this dinner party inside a volcano.

In the years that followed, these overwhelming feelings came back sporadically. Then it became a lot worse around the age of sixteen. The panic occurred anywhere I couldn't leave whenever *I* wanted: restaurants, movie theaters, public transportation, airplanes, waiting rooms, queues, or family get-togethers. I consistently felt as though I was trapped in a cave, and I was always counting down the minutes until I could get out of there.

At first, I thought I had claustrophobia, but that didn't make any sense. I wasn't in a tight cave. After all, movie theaters and supermarkets are big. I was at a loss and didn't get what was wrong with me and why I was feeling this way.

It started to dawn on me that other people played a major role in my feelings. It was their opinion I was afraid of, combined with a severe fear of all of the symptoms I was feeling and a lack of confidence in my body.

"What would they think of me if they saw my anxiety?"
"Wouldn't they think I was weak? Or strange?"
"And what the heck was wrong with me?"
"Why couldn't I be normal like other people and just have fun?"
"Did I have a major disease in my body that doctors couldn't find?"

I felt ashamed.

There was a huge gap between the image I wanted other people to have of me and how I was really feeling.

How was I ever going to be a good dad and husband with a great career if I continued to feel like this?

I just didn't get it.

By the age of eighteen, I had it just about everywhere that was more than five miles from my home, my safe place, my fortress. My social life was reduced to those events I could absolutely not avoid, like going to class. But I always went straight home after.

My list of symptoms had grown to:

- Pounding heart
- Sweating and feeling warm
- Rapid breathing and/or hyperventilating
- Dizziness and vertigo

- Lightheadedness
- Feeling like someone had parked a car on my chest
- Intestinal problems
- Nausea
- My skin getting very red
- Strange tingling sensations in my arms or legs
- Difficulties swallowing and a dry mouth
- Pain in my chest

Honestly, if you look at that list of symptoms, who wouldn't be worried?

These symptoms gave me panic attack after panic attack, and the most frustrating part was that my doctors—I saw many of them—never found anything. I was in good health. They asked me not to worry so much. That solution sounded easy but didn't help.

I started to lose friends quickly. I don't blame them; it wasn't fun hanging out with me at that time. The panic attacks could strike at any moment. Whenever my friends asked me to join them somewhere, I declined, using one of my many excuses I employed at the time.

I had a ton of **fear of the fear**. I was afraid to feel bad again, to be somewhere I couldn't escape when I wanted to. I was continuously checking in on how I felt.

And, on top of that, I developed a social phobia that made me continuously worry about what other people thought of me.

Not all my fears were linked to the presence or absence of other people. The hypochondria became pretty bad as well. I was sure I had a serious disease and no longer trusted my body. Why else was I having all of those symptoms?

My anxiety became chronic, and I came down with generalized anxiety disorder not long after. The moments without anxiety became scarce.

By 2003, I had developed full agoraphobia. I only felt safe in my own house. I chose a safe job, tried to avoid meetings, and basically adapted my entire life to dodge my anxiety as much as possible. That was fun...

I felt so powerless. That powerlessness was one of the most irritating side effects of my anxiety and panic attacks. I believed I never had control over my thoughts, my body, and my surroundings. I felt worse than a penguin in the desert. I didn't know when and if my symptoms and accompanying anxiety would occur and the thought of that made me even more anxious.

You may understand exactly how I felt.

In 2004, the pinnacle year panic attack wise, it got *so* bad that I even had panic attacks in my own bed. I suffered from a generalized anxiety disorder that made me feel anxious all the time.

One night I said, "Look, Geert, that's it! I've had enough of this. I want you to do whatever it takes to get over this. WHATEVER IT TAKES! I want my old life back. I want to live and have fun, and I only live once. This is not the dress rehearsal. This is it!"

I got so motivated that I started to take action. I'll spare you the details of that trial-and-error period, but it was a long process. Over the next few months, I was talking to a ton of panic attack survivors, testing things, trying mental techniques, working out a strategy, and more. Then, by December 2004, I realized I hadn't had a panic attack or disturbing anxiety for months.

I recognized that I hadn't been partaking in my favorite hobby, checking in on how I felt, for a long time.

I still recall going to a movie theater with the two friends I had left and as I sat there, I was waiting for the panic attack that had always come in the past. It didn't. What a victory! It felt better than anything I had ever achieved before.

I was free. The lights started to reappear in all of the areas of my life that had gone dark years before.

If you still suffer from panic attacks, anxiety, or phobias, your victory moment will come. That will be a feeling you'll never forget.

You might wonder why I called my site "I Love Panic Attacks." Well, although they've made me feel very dark and depressed, I feel so blessed and grateful each and every single day since 2004 when I overcame it all. I'm much happier than I would have ever been if it weren't for the panic attacks. I don't take anything for granted.

In 2005, I started to help a couple of people who suffered from panic attacks. I wanted to figure out if what I had done would work for other people as well. When that test was successful and my first clients were able to get on with their lives too, I felt confident that the methods I had developed and used on myself didn't just work on me. I then recorded everything I did and created the first edition of my audio course. Thousands of people from all over the world have followed that audio course, and it is still very successful to this day.

Not everyone could afford it, so I decided to write my first book in 2010 to help an even broader audience. Then, many years later and with more experience under my belt, I updated the audio course and decided to write a new book, the one you're reading now.

No matter what type of anxiety you have, you'll find lots of techniques in this book that you can start to apply right now. They will make you stronger than you've ever been before. I mean that.

I hope you enjoy this book. I'm not a native English speaker, but I found it important to not use a ghostwriter. I wanted to put my heart and soul into it. I wanted to connect with you, personally, through these words. I've been where you are now. I found the way out, and now I'll show it to you.

Are you excited yet? I hope you are. You're about to embark on a journey that will do a lot more than just help you with anxiety and panic attacks. Let's dive in.

Good luck!

Geert

Part 1: The Counterintuitive Truth about Anxiety and Panic Attacks

I've divided this book into three major parts. First, we'll go over the different forms of anxiety and what causes them. We'll need to deal with those causes. In part 2, you'll learn new techniques to tackle unwanted anxiety and stop panic attacks. Then, part 3 will blend everything from the previous sections together so you can feel the full force of it all. Because the goal is achieving *lasting* results.

Finally, the addendum will go over some specific symptoms and situations you may be plagued by and how to deal with them in detail. This is where you'll get the step-by-step blueprints.

Don't skip ahead though.

I understand you are driven to get your life back right away; that's obviously why you bought this book. But please, bear with me. Devour part one first. We'll need to *understand* anxiety in order to then deal with it.

Let's go!

Meet Brian, Debby, Charles, and Monica

Brian, a 34-year-old manager, had a difficult time at work. He had started out his career as an ambitious guy trying to achieve greatness and was well on his way. About seven months ago, while attending a meeting, Brian felt the sudden urge to get out of the meeting room.

His heart rate went up significantly; he got a dry mouth and started to sweat heavily. It felt as if someone had greatly raised the temperature in the room and turned it into a sauna, which didn't make any sense to Brian. Who in their right mind would to this? And why did his colleagues seem unplagued by all that he was feeling? As he tried to pay attention to the presentation, his mind kept worrying about what he was experiencing, how he could excuse himself from the meeting, and what his colleagues and boss would think. He didn't want to ruin the seemingly perfect image they had of him. He had worked hard on that image, for years.

After that one traumatizing moment, his first panic attack, Brian started to dread meetings and desperately tried to avoid them, often coming up with the most ridiculous excuses. If he had to give a presentation himself, he would lie awake at night—days, often weeks in advance. His career was starting to suffer, causing him to miss a couple of promotions. He was no longer on track.

Brian continuously checked in on how he felt and started to suffer from a generalized anxiety disorder. He was anxious from the moment he opened his eyes in the morning till the moment he kissed his wife goodnight.

His wife and friends advised him to "just get over it." They told him he was worrying too much about it all. Although this advice was well intended, it didn't serve him at all.

Debby, on the other hand, had another problem. She's a 41-year-old single mom who used to travel all around the world while she was in her twenties. She drove her car to far-away places, took planes as if they were cabs, and enjoyed the freedom that came with it all. After giving birth to her first daughter, Debby started to notice a reluctance to drive her car. She couldn't pinpoint why, but she began to feel dizzy while driving. While behind the wheel, Debby often felt some nausea and experienced some heart palpitations too. This was frustrating to her since she was starting to lose faith in her ability to get the car, with those in it, home safe.

As the weeks progressed, Debby noticed she had anxiety specifically on highways and bridges, in tunnels, and while stuck in traffic jams. It felt like some form of claustrophobia, but Debby didn't understand why. Her car wasn't an elevator or a cave filled with angry bats and rattlesnakes.

Not long after, she started to feel the same range of sensations in airplanes and other forms of public transportation. This limited her freedom to a great extent as Debby decided to stay home as much as she could. She wanted to avoid feeling like *that.* Driving her kids to school was all she could do and even then her anxiety was extraordinarily high. She feared getting into an accident, especially with the kids in the car.

Charles was only 28 when he was convinced he was very sick. He felt a whole range of strange sensations on a daily basis and couldn't understand why. His doctor and hospital visits didn't help.

"You are in good health, Charles. Go home and stop worrying" was all they said over and over. Charles even called for an ambulance a couple of times because he was sure his heart was giving up on him. Afterward, all of the doctors and nurses told him it was just anxiety. He was too stressed and had to relax more. They tried to prescribe anti-depressants, but he always refused to take them; he was not depressed.

The uncertainty of what he had and what was going on kept him continuously anxious. Charles was certain he was sick.

He searched the web for answers. When Charles found stories of people who were actually sick, he was confident he was also suffering from the same illnesses. This uninformed realization resulted in anxiety spikes that often led to panic attacks. His "illness" was all Charles could think about, and he was searching for reassurance wherever he could. This was starting to weigh heavily on his wife and son, too. Even doctor visits where he was declared to be in great health didn't reassure him like they used to. His wife tried to support him, but she was starting to get frustrated considering nothing she did or tried seemed to help. Charles might as well have been training tigers, because that's what his life was starting to look like—a circus.

Monica only had a few friends, but she enjoyed going out when she was a teenager. As she became older, Monica noticed she felt good when people she knew well surrounded her. People she didn't know, however, made her feel uneasy. Social settings involving large crowds were not at all possible. She had tried it once but immediately became nauseated and lightheaded; her heart raced and her bowels became overactive. Doctors called it "irritable bowel syndrome." Monica started to escape crowds because she always felt like she was about to faint or get tummy troubles in front of others. Avoidance seemed like a good option to keep the anxiety at bay.

As the years went by, avoidance proved to be a bad plan because her anxiety always found her when she tried to play hide-and-seek. The anxiety gradually increased and took over more and more aspects of her life until it was clear she had a social phobia combined with agoraphobia. When too many other people were present, Monica had to run home or at least seek a safe place. Waiting in line, networking, going to weddings, and other seemingly normal activities were no longer possible for her. She was too afraid of feeling bad and didn't want other people to notice her obvious social distress. She was ashamed and frantically tried to uphold the image of a strong woman everyone previously had of her.

These are four stories of people whose lives were seriously limited by the consequences of anxiety. After years of coping with their anxiety and trying to find help, they came to me. They all fully recovered after putting in an effort and mastering the set of powerful techniques presented within this book that can help you overcome unwanted anxiety, panic attacks, and even phobias.

There may be a negative voice in your head saying, "Sure, but *my case* is different. I'm probably not going to get any results. I never do, and I've tried so many times." I already warned you about this. That's just your negative voice talking, and that's exactly the reason why you should read this book. It's one of the causes of anxiety.

And if your anxiety is different from what I just described, please don't despair. These are just a couple of real-life stories out of the thousands I have from my clients.

The Four Stages of a Full Recovery

Recovery always happens in stages.

The first stage you will reach is the one where your intolerance to anxiety will be gone. You'll be participating in whatever it is that currently still makes you uncomfortable. You'll still feel some anxiety, but for many reasons that will become clear when you get to this point, the anxiety won't bother you. The fear of the fear will be gone. That's the first liberation. Feeling the anxiety and no longer letting it rule your life.

Stage two appears when you'll partake in something that previously gave you anxiety, and you'll realize the anxiety and the accompanying sensations simply aren't there. Your anxiety may not be linked to locations or events, and in that case you'll just notice that you haven't had to think of your anxiety for some time. No checking in was needed.

It will feel as if you're forgetting something, forgetting to freak out, that is. This will be a *very* liberating moment, as I'm sure you can imagine.

Then, stage three arises. As you start to enjoy many activities again and can finally go on with your life, you'll arrive at a point where you will become aware of what's been happening, "Huh? I haven't felt anxious for a long time. I don't even remember when the last time was. I've really been enjoying life again. Is it all really in the past now?"

Then comes a very important moment, stage four. This may be months or even years down the road. The moment that the anxiety tries to return. It will. Up until that instant you may have been living your life fully, with clear skies and sunshine every day. Then, a little cloud of anxiety tries to appear. That may sound scary, for now. However, since by that time you'll have finished this entire book, you'll know *exactly* how to respond and the anxiety won't take over. It won't be able to, because you cannot unlearn what you're about to learn. It will be like seeing a long-lost friend passing by, making you remember the past, without going back to it.

Those, in all honesty, are *the* best moments. I don't know what you'll be doing then, but you'll feel a form of gratitude that's hard to explain.

Those are the instants where you'll realize how much your life has changed, how you're able to enjoy it so much more and, like me, will not ever take it all for granted. You'll know then that you became better than the old version of you, and there won't be a way back.

Myths about Anxiety and Panic Attacks

"You Are Weak"

I still recall the pep talks other people gave me when I suffered from debilitating anxiety. "Just get over it. It's all in your head" or even "Man up!" Some would even ask, "Why do you get so worked up over nothing?"

Other phrases I was offered were: "You're just working too hard. You need to relax" and "You're too stressed. Why don't you try some yoga?"

They had no idea what I was going through. They simply didn't get it.

Friends, family, and my girlfriend at the time didn't understand. If I had severely cut my finger while practicing chainsaw juggling, then they would have at least *seen* something was wrong with me. But my brokenness was hidden. They often thought I was imagining it. They presumed I was weak, and some didn't even hide their opinion.

Imagine a soldier running through a terrorist-infested city somewhere in the desert. He's alone and should wait for reinforcements, but he doesn't, being the brave man he is. He keeps going.

As beads of sweat run down his face, he hears gunfire coming from the left and right. He quickly looks up but can't see the shooters. He can hear the bullets fly right by him, and he feels the subtle air stream they create as they swirl past his head, barely missing him. The soldier decides to be strong and to keep going, even though he's terrified and panicking in every way possible.

The question is: is this soldier weak?

Of course not!

This is a picture of what truly debilitating anxiety or panic attacks feel like. You're under fire, but you have no idea where the danger is coming from. Doing whatever it is you fear, even if it's something simple like boarding an airplane or giving a speech, is as brave as the soldier running through a war zone. It launches the same defense systems in your body.

You are not weak. You are, in fact, very brave. What can be a walk in the park to *them* can feel like going to a war zone for you. Even my therapists and psychiatrists didn't really understand. They wanted to help, and I respect them for that. They cared, but to me, it always felt as if they thought I was exaggerating, especially with the pointless techniques they kept suggesting. I got the feeling that they just didn't get it. Even though they meant well.

The longer your anxiety sticks around, the more other people will start to get fed up with your excuses to avoid doing that what you fear. Some might even take it personally and believe you simply don't like *them*.

This can happen to anyone by the way. I've helped people from all walks of life from the big-time CEO to the intern or student whose life is just getting started. I've helped people of all ages, from the 14-year-old whose mother had contacted me to the 84-year-old man who had been living with his anxiety for over fifty years.

Some of my clients are psychiatrists or medical doctors. I've even had an airline pilot once who was afraid of flying. Yes, it happened. And I'm sure you can imagine how ashamed he was to admit this to anyone. "Welcome aboard. This is your captain speaking. Sit back and relax and enjoy the flight. And if there's anyone with a fear of flying, don't worry, you're not alone. I'm scared to death as well!"

You are not weak! Anxiety can strike anyone at any time. When the anxiety system starts to run afoul, it will take over your life... until *you* stop it. And that's why I wrote this book. I want to help *you* deactivate your panic attacks and eliminate your unnecessary anxiety.

The Power Is Already Within You

You won't need a miracle or a wish-granting genie to overcome your anxiety. The power is already within you.

You won't need to change your genes or hire the DeLorean from the movie *Back to the Future* to go back in time and fix something that went wrong. Even though the problem started in the past, we cannot and need not change the past. Talking about the past does not fix panic attacks or anxiety. There are things you are doing now, each and every day, that maintain the anxiety. Those are the true and current causes that you'll have to remove.

Four years ago, a man from France followed my course. He was 84 when he found my website and ordered the French version of my audio course. He had been suffering from severe panic attacks since the age of 29, that's fifty-five years! Six months after starting the audio course, he e-mailed me explaining he had overcome his panic attacks. About a year after, his wife thanked me for giving them the best time of their lives.

Fifty-five years of panic attacks... can you imagine? I didn't prescribe any pills (I'm not a doctor); I didn't use any voodoo or magic spells, and I didn't put on my angel wings since I don't have any. The power was already within him, and it had been all that time. I simply showed him how to use it, just as I'll show you now.

How to Feel Totally Calm During Moments of Intense Anxiety

I bet this title sounds like a dream, doesn't it? What if I were to present you with a formula that would help you to be totally calm, cool, and collected during moments of *intense* anxiety? Would that be something you're interested in?

I bet you are. And this may be the very reason why your anxiety is so persistent!

That's because it is the wrong approach.

I'll dig into the details later, but I wanted to bring up this counterintuitive concept now, because it is so fundamental.

When you suffer from unwanted anxiety, the goal is never to feel calm. The goal is *not* to take your anxiety away. Please allow me to explain since I understand this may sound very odd.

The more you try to make the anxiety go away, the more you try to stay calm, the more you try to make your symptoms disappear, *the worse it will get!*

And I guess I don't even have to prove this. You have already experienced it plenty of times or you wouldn't be reading this book.

The more the anxiety upsets you, the more power you give it.

Trying to avoid anxiety or attempting to make it vanish is a form of resistance, and the anxiety you're feeling already *represents* resistance to something that's happening or that you were thinking about. That's what launched the anxiety in the first place. Hence, the more resistance you add, the more you forcefully try to be calm, the more nervous you will get.

It's the equivalent of pouring gasoline on a fire in an effort to extinguish the flames. Or trying to fall asleep by frantically hoping you will fall asleep soon. How well does that work?

When you are anxious, your nervous system is already freaking out. We shouldn't increase the pressure.

This was one of the many mistakes I was making in the past. I'll explain more later, but I wanted to set this straight from the start.

Goal number one is not to take your anxiety away; that happens at a later stage. First, we'll need to work on your intolerance to anxiety because that's the true root cause of what you're currently dealing with.

For now, remember that one of the most calming emotions you can give yourself is realizing that it is OK to let go of control, to let things flow and just see what happens. *Even when what you are experiencing is as pleasant as an unwanted hug from a stranger who forgot to shower or apply deodorant for the last seven months.*

The more you fight anxiety, the worse it will get. The more you let go, the faster it will pass.

Easier said than done, of course. Let's try to make it as easy as possible.

Why Are We So Anxious?

How did this happen? You're smart. You're doing the best you can, trying to make something of your life. And then, all of a sudden, anxiety tries to ruin it all.

It often starts out small. One event, one little thing where it rears its ugly head and shows you what it's capable of.

Then, like any sane human being would, you think, "Well, I hope *that* doesn't happen again" and the fear of the fear is born.

This attitude then sets a chain of events in motion where, through a slow process, anxiety will try to dominate your life more and more. Oftentimes there will be things you used to do without blinking that now make you lie awake at night weeks before the event. At that point, anxiety starts to overshadow everything.

If you suffer from anxiety, you are not alone. According to the Anxiety and Depression Association of America (ADAA) and the National Institute of Mental Health, an estimated 18% of the population suffers from anxiety-related issues, with or without panic attacks.[1]

Many people who have contacted me over the years believed their anxiety was unique, that there was something wrong with them. I was no different. It honestly even took me a long time finding out that it *was* anxiety disturbing me, for at first I simply believed there was a major, overlooked issue within my body.

---

[1] https://www.nimh.nih.gov/health/statistics/prevalence/any-anxiety-disorder-among-adults.shtml

Whatever it is you fear, whatever your thoughts, you are not alone. You are not broken, and there is nothing wrong with the chemical substances in your brain. I've heard it all during the more than a decade of helping people with anxiety and panic attacks.

I've been there too. I thought I was the only one with those weird thoughts and reactions I used to suffer from. You are not abnormal. You're just being flooded by negative thoughts that, for now, you choose to follow and put emphasis upon.

The reason why you may feel unique is because you can't see anxiety, let alone anxious thoughts. I have some famous celebrities in my client list and, upon looking at their public lives, you cannot imagine the anxieties they face. They seem (and are) very strong, yet they too are burdened with unwanted anxiety, unwanted thoughts and feelings they'd rather avoid. I once had a famous violin player as a client who had panic attacks during her concerts. The audience and even I couldn't see it. Yet, she was in the midst of dealing with a full-blown panic attack.

Everyone has anxiety to some extent, a lot of people have panic attacks, and some people you've been in the same room with have had a panic attack while you were present. They were simply really good at hiding it, just as you undoubtedly are or at least try to be. Not everyone feels comfortable openly talking about them. We'll talk about this sense of shame later in the book, because that's an important part of the problem too.

Defining Anxiety

Let's first look at what anxiety is. Anxiety is a simple self-defense mechanism built into your body to steer clear of a danger or to react in the most appropriate way when we are faced with an imminent threat.

This means that anxiety is a simple emotion. I don't want to downplay the enormous effect uncontrollable anxiety can have on our lives; I lived it for fourteen years. Nevertheless, it's a simple emotion meant to save our life, that's it.

This system came in handy on a daily basis until about one hundred years ago, when daily life was life-or-death dangerous.

Imagine a version of yourself four hundred years ago. You're alone and walking around in a wooded area. As you're walking, you suddenly hear the rustling of leaves. You turn around and see two men approaching. They are armed with weapons and the look on their faces makes your stomach turn. You quickly try to hide behind a tree without making too much noise. As these men walk past you, you sigh with relief and continue your journey.

Not long after this encounter, you notice some movement to your right. You instantly realize it's a brown bear with cubs walking through the woods. Your anxiety rises again, and you slowly and quietly step away. Because of your swift action, the bear won't see you; you get to live another day. In a span of thirty minutes, your anxiety system saved your life, twice.

Until not so long ago, our anxiety systems were necessary on a daily basis. We faced physical threats and many possible dangers to our lives, and we had to constantly be on guard.

That system is still active and alive in us today. Like radar, it scans your surroundings and analyzes what you see, hear, and yes, it even scans what you *think*. The anxiety self-defense system can be induced in many ways, both on a gut-level reaction without having to think (a part of our brain called the amygdala takes care of this) and by using thoughts that often start with "what if?"

Having one "what if?" thought can be all that's needed to launch the anxiety and self-defense system.

As you are anxious, your body can go into a variety of modes. It will most often go into some form of fight-or-flight status. As a result, your muscles will receive more blood in order for you to fight the threat or run away from the danger. Your heart rate will go up, your digestion will cease, less blood will go to your brain leading to dizziness or light-headedness, you will get a dry mouth, your breathing pattern will change, and so on. You'll feel a whole range of unusual sensations. The same ones you would feel after running as fast as you could for about one hundred yards. Only this time, you might not have been moving at all.

If you met an angry bear you would probably not mind feeling any of these strange sensations. All of your energy would presumably go to freaking out about the bear, not the sensations and the anxiety itself.

Now imagine what happens if you're just involved in your daily activities and start feeling any of these strange sensations *then*... what then?

Chances are you *will* worry about what you're feeling. It doesn't make any sense for you to have racing thoughts, feel the anxiety in your stomach, have a rapid heartbeat, or any of the other symptoms that accompany anxiety. That's when anxiety, a generalized anxiety disorder, panic attacks, and phobias can start to take over your life.

The anxiety will start to pop up more and more, as if it's playing hide-and-seek. It will seem to spread like a virus that you frantically try to avoid. The reason is simple. This is yet *another* self-defense system. Whenever you've felt anxious somewhere or when anxiety hit you while you were doing something, your mind remembered. Consciously or not, you made a mental note: "That was dangerous. That was life threatening. Let's avoid this place or doing *that* in the future."

These are the wonders of our amygdala and other "let's live another day" systems. The next time you go to a similar place, the anxiety will start to rise automatically. Sometimes even thinking about it will be enough to make you anxious, especially when you know you have to do that what you fear in the future. As the moment comes closer, your mind will go into anticipation mode, reviewing and fretting about all of the possible outcomes and imagining how that day will be a disaster. That's when the "what if?" thinking starts, my favorite hobby in the era of my anxiety and panic attacks.

What your body and mind are doing in this case is telling you, "Hey, last time you were here, you met that angry bear, remember? Be on your guard! I'll be preparing you, just in case."

Again, a very handy system when life was super dangerous. But when your mind tries to warn you about an upcoming flight, a meeting, the checkout counter, that wedding party, or whatever it is you dislike at the moment... it's not so handy.

On top of this, the system that's trying to regulate everything, your nervous system, is getting so worn out and tired that it will make your anxious reactions grow exponentially. That's why I'll spend a significant amount of time on what you can do to desensitize your nervous system, so it can heal.

A Different World

We, as a society, are more anxious than ever because our anxiety systems are malfunctioning. Life isn't as dangerous as it was a couple of generations ago and yet our bodies haven't adapted. The alarm keeps ringing and continues to classify events as dangerous when they aren't.

We, on the other hand, are faced with many pressures and non-lethal dangers like meeting a deadline, making enough money, keeping up with the Joneses, paying back the mortgage, having the best possible career while being the best possible wife/husband/mother/father/boyfriend/girlfriend/pet-owner and more... pressures our ancestors never had to deal with. All of these stressors and "oh no!" moments launch our anxiety systems over and over again while there is no *real* threat.

The way we live plays a role in this too. E-mails and stress-related work stuff follow us around like a boomerang. Our smartphones now offer continuous busyness. We're constantly bombarded with urgent e-mails or new (social) messages; these may cause little stress spikes giving you the urge to check your phone over and over again, thus stressing your nervous system even more.

Our work, our to-do lists, and other peoples' wishes follow us around everywhere. The only place we were free from work-related stress and people's immediate demands was flying high up in the air. Unfortunately, even that has been invaded with the introduction of Wi-Fi on planes a little over a decade ago.

This is not a rant, mind you. It is the way our society is evolving, and there's nothing we can do to stop it. There are many advantages, too. We nevertheless have to adapt and do it fast. If we don't, more and more people will suffer from anxieties, burnouts, and other stress-related illnesses every year.

Thankfully, you *can* learn how to adapt and change.

A Choice

As you'll learn, a major cause of anxiety is the way we interpret what's happening around us—the story we tell ourselves whenever something happens. Good news! We have control over these stories, and we *can* change the impact they have upon us.

This is not my personal invention. Many great thinkers have been battling and overcoming anxiety and other emotional challenges for centuries. The first one that comes to mind is the great Roman Emperor Marcus Aurelius (161-181 A.C.E). He wrote in his journal, *"You have power over your mind, not outside events. Realize this, and you will find strength."*

Victor Frankl, the great doctor and psychologist who was captured by the Nazis during WWII, learned many lessons while he was humiliated and starved in a concentration camp. He discovered how to enjoy himself even though he was in one of the most horrendous places on earth. He described in his book *Man's Search for Meaning,* "Everything can be taken from a man but one thing: the last of the human freedoms— to choose one's attitude in any given set of circumstances, to choose one's own way."

Claire Weekes, the Australian general practitioner who specialized in anxiety, also kept explaining to her patients that the solution lay in true acceptance because that's the only way to calm down the nervous system that's causing all the havoc.

It *is* all a choice, as overly simplistic as that may sound, for now. Here too I don't want to downplay your anxiety. But it is crucial that we see it for what it really is.

It is never the symptoms or the location and situation you're in that cause anxiety and panic attacks. It is your response to them that matters. One person's heart skips a beat, and she doesn't even notice it. Or she does and goes on with her day. Yet another woman with the exact same symptom can end up in terror with a pure panic attack while Googling what it could all mean... because *she* chose to get scared of the symptom.

One person can be in a major traffic jam, in the longest tunnel you can imagine, and be lip-syncing to a popular Taylor Swift song about one of her many ex-boyfriends as loudly as he can. While another man can sit there in the exact same situation, with sweat dripping down his forehead, heart pounding through his chest, fingers gripping his steering wheel like he's holding onto a ledge because *he* chose to agree with his "I can't get away here! I'm stuck! Help!" thoughts.

It is a choice! And if you suffer from anxiety with or without panic attacks, you've simply made a habit out of making the wrong choice. This, luckily, can be changed.

Let me give you a simple example. You're driving to an important meeting, and you're running late. You unexpectedly end up in a traffic jam on the highway, and there are no exits the next couple of miles. What do you do?

If your mind automatically thinks, "Oh no, I'm going to be late. I'll never make it, and my colleagues/boss will be mad. Why oh why did I leave so late? This always happens to me!"

Guess what? You'll be pumping yourself up, and before you know it, you'll try to telepathically make all of those cars in front of you move out of the way, which they probably won't do. Your heart rate will go up; your face will turn red, and you'll be pushing yourself into the fight-or-flight state because you're communicating to your body that there is a major threat. As a result, you will feel absolutely terrible. When you finally arrive at work, you'll be exhausted even before you start dealing with the consequences of your tardiness. This is the path you chose, and the resulting emotions you'll feel are the consequences.

That said, it *is* a choice.

There is another approach to this situation. Your mind might say, "Well, there you have it. I won't make it. I might as well not stress about it since pumping myself up and getting anxious won't give my car wings or make the other cars vanish. So be it. I'll deal with the consequences when I get there. For now, I'm going to listen to my favorite playlist, sit back, and relax." If that's the path you choose, you'll be totally calm when you arrive at work. You'll be ready to deal with the consequences as best as you can.

The outside environment is the same in both cases. The traffic jam will make you late, and whoever is waiting for you might still get mad. However, your emotions, your happiness, and your entire nervous system will get a totally different treatment based on the thoughts you choose to focus upon. It is a choice—a hard one at first, a simple one with practice.

Later on in this book, I will give you techniques to make this choice more effectively, and of course not just in traffic jams. And after a while, your mind will start to automatically choose the correct response because you will have reprogrammed it to do so.

But for now, let's dig a bit deeper into what happens when you're anxious.

The Vicious Cycle

When anxiety is dominating your life, it didn't happen overnight. It creeps in and starts to take over little by little even though it may seem to have started suddenly.

As we've just seen, anxiety is a simple but vital self-defense mechanism in our bodies. It is meant to point out the danger and to help you take care of it. We can avoid that danger or deal with it when avoidance is no longer an option.

Just imagine you and I are going for a walk in the jungle. As we're enjoying the beautiful flowers, butterflies, and sunshine, we hear a sound in front of us. We see something orange and furry. As if we're hit by lightning, we get an instant adrenaline shot and realize it's a tiger, a hungry one.

The fight-or-flight system kicks in. Our hearts start to pound really fast, and blood is rushed to our muscles so we can run away from the tiger or stay and fight. As a consequence of this, we might feel nauseated, sweaty, dizzy, and overall pretty bad and super nervous. Our blood is primarily going to our muscles; so non-vital organs are put on pause, for now.

This is the fight-or-flight response in full action. An instantaneous reaction where our amygdala, a part of our brain, decides there's a danger.

The word "instantaneous" is important here.

We don't get the time to consciously think, "Oh, look! Tony the tiger. Does it represent a danger? Is it in a bad mood? Should I go and cuddle with it? Should I negotiate with it and explain the benefits of becoming a vegetarian? Should I run?" There's no time for any of that. Our amygdala says, "Better safe than sorry!" and launches the fight-or-flight response right away. This can give you an avalanche of symptoms and strange sensations.

Now at that time, if we're standing in the jungle with a hungry tiger eyeballing us, we're not going to say, "Hey, wow! Look at that. My heart is pounding really fast. Am I about to have a heart attack? And you know, I'm super dizzy too. That can't be normal. Let me Google that!" No, of course not, that won't happen! There is no Wi-Fi in the jungle!

All kidding aside, the danger is clear and right in front of us. The tiger will get your *full* and undivided attention. Chances are we're not even going to notice or worry about those sensations. We know *why* we're anxious.

The problem starts when you're just minding your own business and driving around in your car, sitting in a meeting room, eating at a restaurant, talking in a social setting, shopping for groceries, or even sitting home alone and all of a sudden you sense that first sensation, that first symptom.

That is the first and crucial part.

If you're like I was, your mind starts to wonder what's going on and why you're feeling this way. Those are anxious thoughts, aren't they? You're adding a layer of anxiety and thus pushing down the first domino block. You're communicating to your body that there seems to be some kind of danger—you do this by having those anxious thoughts and focusing on them—and your body says, "No problem. I have a fight-or-flight response for dangers, so here goes. I'll give you some adrenaline, thank me later!"

As a direct result of the adrenaline, your symptoms and anxiety level increase. You'll get more nervous and anxious. But there's still no real tiger in front of you. Your mind probably then thinks, "Wow, seriously, I feel even worse! What's going on? Should I call someone? How do I get out of here? Where are the exits? What will people think of me? Who can help me?"

Would you agree these are even more anxious thoughts? They are. So, yes, you're adding *another* layer of anxiety, and you're communicating to your body, "Look, there's not just one tiger in front of me. I've just been dropped into an arena filled with tigers that have been drooling over a picture of me for months, and I think someone just dropped a couple of scorpions in my shirt too! Heeeeelp!"

Your body says, "No worries. Really. There's more where that came from. Here is some more adrenaline. Let me crank up that fight-or-flight response so you can fight that major danger and survive this! Now go, fight for your life!" And all of your symptoms will increase even more.

More dominos start to fall, and you then launch a vicious anxiety and panic attack cycle. If you continue this thought process, you *will* launch a panic attack.

For some people, their anxiety is location driven (e.g., fearing a supermarket or somewhere where you can't get away whenever you want); it can be the fear of doing something (e.g., driving, crossing a bridge, going through a tunnel, giving a speech, being the center of attention, going crazy), or it can be the fear of feeling something (e.g., fearing a sensation in your body and believing something bad is about to happen to you) making you continuously scan your body for aches and pains, also called checking in. And yet another group feels seemingly anxious for no reason whatsoever.

If this continues for a couple of weeks or months, you'll probably get fear of the fear, where you'll do everything you can to avoid feeling that way again. As if you're allergic to the anxiety itself.

This is the very root of the problem!

Every single living being experiences anxiety and fear. People with panic attacks or generalized anxiety problems, however, fear the anxiety itself. They have a profound intolerance to anxiety, and this is what fuels the anxiety-virus that will then slowly start to take over each and every part of their lives.

So step one, if you want to overcome anxiety-related problems, is to work on your intolerance to the anxiety. That's exactly what we will do too. But we won't stop there.

Being free from unwanted anxiety simply means that you generally are in a happy state without the never-ending need to check-in on how you feel, on whether the anxiety or the dreaded symptoms will come or not.

Because indeed, as the anxiety-virus spreads, the dominos can then start to fall in other areas of your life. It started on New Year's Eve for me, then advanced to restaurants, university classes, movie theaters, cars, meeting rooms, well... until I got agoraphobia and stayed home as much as I could. And as soon as something I feared was planned on my calendar, I'd be anticipating it for weeks in advance. Until the dreaded day passed. I would then feel good for a day or so, until my amygdala found the next event to focus upon. It was a never-ending rollercoaster ride of anxiety and fear.

As you've already read, these results are part of a self-defense system that makes a mistake and misjudges the danger. There is no real danger. Your body, however, doesn't know that. Your negative thoughts keep telling that system there is something to be afraid of, and this launches the vicious panic-attack cycle I just described. You'll learn how to reverse that throughout this book. You'll learn to turn off the fire alarm and more importantly, how to not push the alarm button in the first place.

It's not all about fight or flight

There are subsystems of anxiety serving other causes. A small percentage of people get depersonalization, where they feel they've just left their body... as if they're no longer present or dreaming. Everything just feels unreal. This is yet another self-defense system, assisting you when it's too late, when there's no point in running or fighting.

David Livingstone, the famous adventurer, was one of the first to describe it. A lion had jumped on top of him and had already handed out the first bites. Yet Livingstone couldn't feel a thing. He was fully at peace and time seemed to slow down.

Isn't that strange?

His body decided it was too late to fight. If you get bitten and your heart is pumping like crazy, then you'll lose more blood, and your chances of survival go down. So, if it's too late to fight anyway, why not sit back and relax and just see *if* you survive it? With this system, everything slows down, and your body releases endorphins instead of the fight-or-flight adrenaline.

Great system in the event that you ever find a lion on your back, but you can imagine it's pretty scary if you have an out-of-body experience while you're not physically wounded. But here too, it's simply a self-defense system that is misfiring.

When you have a panic attack or a strong moment of anxiety, unless you see a predator about to eat you or become aware of another physical and imminent danger, you are safe. Everything you're feeling doesn't mean something is wrong.

It's just a false alarm. It's an adrenaline rush, the same kind you'd feel during a rollercoaster ride.

Strange as that may sound, please try to admire those systems. This will help you to not get scared when they kick in, so you can convince your body more easily that it's a false alarm instead of making it worse by listening to your negative voice. It's always a bad idea to add more anxiety whenever the anxiety system is launched and there is no life-or-death threat in front of you. Otherwise, you'll be pushing on even more alarm buttons.

"Don't worry, everything is fine, I am fine... right?"

Before we can move on to what you *should* do when you're anxious, we need to spend some time on what doesn't work, so you can stop doing *that* first and cease pouring gasoline onto the fire.

Everyone who's anxious is looking for reassurance. That's what we've been doing ever since we were kids. "Daddy, are you *sure* there is not a monster in my closet?" Reassurance temporarily takes the anxiety away. But it is not the solution. Since shortly after the mind goes: "What if the monster is hiding under the bed instead of the closet?"

Off we go again...

Reassurance is pushing the anxiety away through the left window, only to see it re-enter a while later through the right window. It just doesn't work.

I personally used the interwebs to find reassurance. I wanted to know that the symptoms I was feeling were OK. I came home empty handed every single time because I always found more proof that I should indeed agonize.

Some people love to call someone for some emotional support.

And most, if not all, try to reassure themselves by repeating, "Everything is fine. This is not *so* bad. I am fine."

This, as I'm sure you've experienced, doesn't work either. It's a lie. And if there's one person we should never lie to, then it's ourselves. Clearly, everything is not fine, or you wouldn't be feeling anxious.

Reassurance gives more power to the emotion of anxiety. You think, "I'm fine" and then get another thought or sensation proving that you're not, hence putting oil on the fire.

The true solution lies in concluding that even when what's happening is not fine (and thus acknowledging it), you are OK with it. That's the way to avoid raising the already present level of anxiety. We'll extensively look at this later on.

Let's first go over all of the symptoms you may feel when the anxiety rises.

Symptoms

Anxiety and especially panic attacks come with a whole list of symptoms and strange bodily sensations that will probably make you uneasy and possibly give you a panic attack.

Some of the most common ones are:

- A general sense of nervousness or jitteriness
- Increased heart rate
- Heart skips a beat
- Light-headedness
- Nausea
- Dizziness
- Tingling sensations
- Sweating
- Getting a flushed face
- Dry mouth
- Sweating
- Tightness in the chest
- Headache
- Digestive issues
- Blurred vision or inability to focus
- Trembling
- The inability to calm down / *constant* nervousness

This is not an exhaustive list, but these are the most common symptoms that accompany panic attacks and anxiety. Do note that if you suffer from these symptoms, it's best to have your health checked by a doctor. When she or he doesn't find anything then you can deal with the anxiety that's causing them.

Good Versus Bad Anxiety

Wow, this title probably got you thinking, "Wait what? Is there such a thing as *good* anxiety?" Sure there is! You are still alive today because of your anxiety.

I once lived in a house where the garden was overgrown by all sorts of plants and trees.

Wildcats plagued our area at that time, and for some reason, they loved the jungle I called my garden. When one of those wild cats gave birth to her kittens, I could observe them from my kitchen and living room. Every nest of kittens had a variety of personalities. In each nest, I could see two extremes: the fearless and the fearful. Some kittens proudly looked out over the entire village from the top of one of my trees without caring about the way down, mere months after they were born; and the other kittens with too much anxiety ran for the hills when an angry-looking pigeon flew over.

As they grew up, the fearless kittens took more and more risks, unaware of the possible dangers. Maybe they were aware, but they simply didn't care. What became poignantly clear to me was that the fearless kittens never grew up. They didn't make it. They failed to see the danger even when it was right in front of them.

The other kittens, from the very fearful ones to the normal ones, survived each and every time.

In the line of your ancestors, you'll find people who had at least a moderate amount of fear. That's why they survived and were able to procreate. Remember, even as little as three to four generations back, life was still very dangerous on a daily basis. Fearless people simply didn't make it. They were blind to the dangers that could (and often did) kill them. Your great-great grandparents had a well-functioning fear system that kept them alive, and it's because of your anxiety system that you too are still alive today. It has continuously shown you the dangers and warned you of the real threats you encountered.

It would be silly to try to go for a life with no anxiety at all. We will nevertheless work on your intolerance to anxiety and try to get rid of the illogical anxiety. Most importantly, however, you'll learn to make a distinction between good and bad anxiety.

Good Anxiety

This is legitimate anxiety. Your "let's stay alive as long as possible" radar saw something, and it turns out this might be a true danger. Good anxiety also includes being on edge for events that would give anyone some stress because they are truly important and outside of your comfort zone. This type of anxiety is what some would call fear. Fear is a legitimate form of anxiety.

Examples are:

- Going for a walk in the woods where bears live and deciding to not use the honey-scented face cream you normally apply.

- Deciding you are too tired to continue to drive and pulling over to sleep in a motel or at least take a rest.

- Feeling some nerves because you're giving a very important presentation to some people who seem like they couldn't care less.

- Being a bit on edge before walking on stage to give a speech.

- Deciding to stay in the boat and not go for a swim with your inflatable dolphin after you saw a shark fin emerge.

- Being a bit anxious when moving to a new state or country to start the next chapter in your life

- Feeling some nerves when getting married, starting a new job, becoming a parent, making a serious investment, giving your resignation, being let go, filing for divorce, etc.

Good anxiety cannot and should not be avoided. Sure, it would be awesome if you could go to a major job interview that can make or break your career without even a hint of anxiety. That won't happen though. You're human just like the rest of us. The trick here is to not let that anxiety hold you back, to not allow it to stop you or interfere with giving it all you've got. You'll learn how to do that later on.

For now, make a mental note that some forms of anxiety are OK, and that the goal cannot be to avoid anxiety altogether. If anxiety is present, it's best to pick it up and take it with you. _Good_ anxiety can be your companion. It makes you perform better.

Do you remember the fight-or-flight cycle I explained? That very first hint of anxiety you feel can be a performance booster. There's a point later on in the cycle where anxiety will become debilitating and shall severely decrease your performance. That first hint of anxiety, however, is great. It's what every great performer, athlete, businessman or woman, actress/actor, and so on feels before they walk up on stage, into the meeting room, or onto the sports field. That first notion of anxiety makes you mentally more alert; it will help you to think quicker and be more effective.

It will nevertheless be crucial to not let the anxiety increase to the tipping point, where good anxiety can turn into bad anxiety.

Bad Anxiety

This is debilitating anxiety that prevents you from enjoying your life. If you are intolerant to anxiety, good anxiety can turn into bad anxiety pretty quickly.

Bad anxiety is like having a very fast sports car at your disposal, but you're always putting your foot on the brakes and never get to experience the pure and exhilarating power it has.

Bad anxiety can originate from good anxiety that you increase by the games your mind will play or by other forms of negative thinking. Bad anxiety can also emerge on its own based on previous bad experiences that your brain remembered.

Bad anxiety has no basis. It is the fear of a danger that is not real. Bad anxiety is a mistake; it's not meant to happen. It doesn't serve any goal besides destroying the quality of your life and putting your foot on the brake.

Bad anxiety has many side effects. Some examples are:

- Fearing and avoiding social gatherings
- Avoiding networking events where you won't know anyone
- Avoiding bridges, highways, tunnels, driving, flying
- Feeling a strange and rising form of anxiety as you increase the distance from your house or other safe place
- Not wanting to drive more than X miles away from home
- Avoiding crowds
- Avoiding being alone
- Fearing certain thoughts that you try to not have
- Freaking out when you feel a certain sensation or symptom in your body
- Freaking out because you have certain thoughts that you deem as "not normal"
- Not wanting to work out because then your heart rate will go up, you'll get a ton of sensations and you don't like them
- Limiting your career because you fear change
- Limiting your career because you feel like an imposter, as if people will find out you don't belong there at that level
- Relationship troubles because you become needy or jealous too easily

This is, of course, in no way an exhaustive list. Your mind is so creative that you can fear just about anything you can imagine.

It's clear that this is the form of anxiety we'll need to work on. I'll focus a lot on how to deal with good anxiety, how to prevent it from becoming bad anxiety, and how to swipe bad anxiety off the table later on in this book.

Please don't skip ahead though since it's important we lay the foundation first. That's what we are doing now. Part of what will help you overcome your anxieties and panic attacks is the knowledge you're getting right now in part one.

Causes of Anxiety

Now that you know how the anxiety system functions, let's go over the most important causes of anxiety, so you can start to eliminate some of them. Good anxiety has a very clear and simple cause: something real is threatening your life, your health, or someone or something you care about. The danger or the enemy in these cases is clear and the threat is *imminent!* It is real; it's 100% certain that the bad thing will happen and the fight-or-flight will be needed, right now. Just about anyone else put in that same situation would feel anxiety and fear.

But what causes the different forms of abnormal, bad anxiety I've been discussing throughout this book so far? Some people think it's hereditary, or that it's caused by a trauma that happened in the past, a trauma they spend weeks or months digging after in therapy. Others have been told by their doctor they have a chemical imbalance in their brain that can *only* be fixed by taking anti-depressants.

Well, it turns out there are a myriad of possible causes. The more present, the higher the chances that you will suffer from anxiety and possibly even panic attacks. That's why there isn't a cure-all for anxiety and panic attacks. That's why medications fail to deliver adequate long-term results. This is also the reason why digging in your past to find the cause won't get you very far either. Anxiety is induced by many little causes that, all combined, will turn your smile upside down.

In what follows, I'll go over these causes, critique some faulty reasons you should not pay attention to, and give you some techniques to deal with them before we dive into the major anxiety busters in part two. We're almost there.

Let me repeat that there's nothing wrong with you. You might have wondered why you're not like other people who seemingly have fun all the time, go out, have great experiences, and simply don't suffer from anxiety. We both know *those people* only share perfect and often staged moments from their lives. Nobody feels perfect all the time; nobody has the perfect life. That said, there are indeed people out there who can better deal with anxiety than you can at this time.

As you're reading through what follows, whenever you realize I'm talking about you or something you do, please write it down—preferably in a journal that you'll use throughout this book. What you recognize and write down *will* be one of your causes then, one you'll need to pay attention to in the future as you'll be overcoming your unwanted anxiety. Every cause pushes you toward anxiety to some extent (some more than others). The more causes you stack upon one another, the higher the chances of developing an anxiety disorder and getting panic attacks. The more causes you eliminate, the brighter the skies will be again.

Your Body

While I was overcoming my panic attacks, this part is what took me the longest to figure out. When I grew up, I drank a bottle of Coke per day. I even had one next to my bed. Water was for fish, I thought. I ate a bag of Doritos every day and anything else I wanted. Everyone else did it too according to the commercials I saw on TV, so who was I to be different?

When I talked to my doctor about my panic attacks, he never ever asked me what I ate or drank. Then one day my dog Amadeus got sick. He had a swollen head and wasn't his happy self. I took him to the vet right away.

As I put Amadeus on the table for further examination, the vet asked what I had been feeding him, before he even checked him out. Puzzled, I answered the question. It turned out I was giving Amadeus too many treats and leftovers that weren't supposed to be for dogs. Even though his weight was fine, it was creating inflammation and problems in his body.

"If nutrition can have bad effects on my dog," I thought, "I'm sure what I eat will have significant effects on me too. So why did my own doctor never ask me what I ate and drank?" Take it from me and the thousands of people I've been able to help; what you eat and drink has a *major* impact on your body and how you feel!

Yes. Your anxiety and panic attacks may partially be caused by what you are eating and drinking. And we're not talking about calories and your weight here. What you consume has a profound effect on your *emotions* and feelings. Just look at what alcohol can do to people. I'll give you a big one right away:

Caffeine

Caffeine will raise your stress level, will make your nervous system more sensitive, will mess with your body clock, and in short, will act like adrenaline in your body. It is also one of the major causes of adrenal fatigue.[2]

---

[2] For further reading, I suggest *Adrenal Fatigue* by Dr. Wilson.

Caffeine will keep you sharp, alert, and super focused. That's great for some of the population that would otherwise be sleepwalking. But people more prone to anxiety like you and I will get so sensitive and tense that it won't take a lot to get actual anxiety and even a panic attack. Small amounts of caffeine in itself will probably not cause the panic attack; it will just make it super easy to get one!

That's one of the reasons why chocolate should be off limits too; even pure 100% cacao. It not only contains caffeine, it also has amounts of theobromine, a substance that can raise your heart rate and make you jittery.

If you're currently consuming more than two cups of coffee, tea, or anything else with caffeine per day, gradually decrease your intake to zero. Don't go cold turkey or you'll suffer from pretty bad headaches for a couple of days.

And if you think, "Nah, that can't be it! I've been drinking it for ages." Please prove me wrong by giving it a try. Go to zero for four weeks and then introduce it, you'll feel straight away what caffeine has been doing to you.

The Elastic Comfort Circle and Avoidance

The comfort circle is like an elastic band that can be stretched out yet will become smaller again when you stop pushing its boundaries.

Everything inside of your personal comfort circle feels totally normal and doesn't require you to deal with any fears or anxieties. Simple things like brushing your teeth and getting water to boil are within your circle, I hope. Clipping the toenails of wild alligators probably is not.

Everything that's outside of the circle requires a more serious effort. It's new, uncertain, or even downright scary to you. Learning to cross a busy intersection when you were driving a car for the first time was, at that time, outside of your comfort circle. And now, if the fear of driving is not your fear, driving in all kinds of traffic patterns falls well within the circle.

If you want to be comfortable doing anything that's currently outside of your comfort circle, you'll need to put in an effort and stretch the edge of the circle. This is hard, because the closer you get to the edge, the bigger the anxiety and resistance will grow. Your body is trying to warn you of the potential danger. The trick then is to feel the anxiety but not be stopped by it. Keep persisting.

Most of the fun in life lies on the other side of that fear.

This is why **avoidance is a cause of anxiety and panic attacks.** Avoidance is merely a short-term solution. If doing X gave you anxiety or a panic attack, what better way to not have a new panic attack than by avoiding performing X ever again, right?

This is not the solution as we've seen. Your comfort circle, given that it is elastic, will get smaller and smaller. More and more events or experiences will start to scare you, consequently you will have to avoid them too and before you know it even replacing a roll of toilet paper might raise your anxiety. This is a downward spiral and one of the biggest mistakes I made myself. It was the reason why what started with tiny moments of anxiety eventually gave me full agoraphobia where I stayed at home as much as I possibly could. As I was avoiding what scared me, the elastic comfort circle was rapidly closing in on me.

Avoiding whatever scares you gives it power. Power it should not have! By avoiding it, you're acknowledging that it is indeed dangerous and that the anxiety is legitimate. That's exactly the opposite of the solution.

I understand avoidance can be very rewarding. It has the instant miracle effect that it can take your anxiety away and prevent panic attacks.

Trying to control everything belongs to this chapter as well since it is a form of avoidance. "I must make sure I have an aisle seat" or "OK, I'll go, but I must be sure that there are restrooms nearby" or "Before I say yes, let me Google street view the entire location so I can prepare" or "OK as long as someone is with me or is standing by so I can call them." You can fool yourself into believing everything will be fine because you can meticulously foresee and plan every possible outcome, every possible thing that could go wrong. But what if you *still* miss something?

Well, the good news is your life will never ever be boring if you live it with that mindset of trying to have everything under control. Needless to say, this will directly feed your anxiety and will wear out your sensitive nervous system even more. Things will almost never go as planned.

But the deeper message I'd like to pass on is that there is no need to even *have* everything under control. It is not the location, the situation, or even the people that creates the anxiety and possibly the panic attack. It is you and I. We do it with our thoughts.

Having everything under control doesn't help you to control the actual anxiety, it merely gives you a few less reasons to launch the anxiety alarm. But it's still there, and it will be very sensitive as soon as something doesn't go as planned, which will always happen.

There is a better way, and we will deal with it in part two of the book. For now, please understand that the concept of controlling everything and staying within your comfort circle to avoid anxiety are major causes of *generalized anxiety*.

Shame, the underlying cause

As I was sitting in a restaurant with some colleagues, the waiter placed my plate in front of me. Delicious odors of the *tagliatelle frutti di mare* I had ordered wafted to my nostrils. I took a bite and enjoyed it. Then, seconds later, a wave of nausea entered my body. My stomach refused all further service, and my mouth started to water. "Am I going to throw up?" I wondered anxiously.

Let's take a step back. The nausea seems to be the cause of the panic that was about to descend upon me.

But was it really?

"Djeezs, why is this happening now? And look, my plate is still SO full. I can't stop eating now! If I do the waiter is going to ask me what was wrong with it. I'm going to hurt the feelings of the chef! Well provided this was not a frozen dinner he just warmed up, but still, my colleagues... Look at them eating away! Why am I not like *them*? They're having fun and are enjoying this... What if I now have to throw up right here? That's the end of my career for sure. That's the end of my dignity! My other option is to ask to be excused and run to the restrooms. But still, that's not perfect either because *who does that in the middle of his meal?* And my mom always warned me to never run in restaurants! Come on, Geert, that's not normal behavior, and these are no longer normal thoughts to have! Be frickin' normal for a change! It's getting worse, I'm going to have to do something about it. How can I best hide it?"

This would go on and on, and every time the nausea subsided a bit I would take a bite to eat... if it didn't subside I would indeed take a break and tell them I wasn't well. The problem was I was never well when we ate out, nor when I ate in a group setting elsewhere.

The nausea was just an unpleasant symptom, often caused by certain ingredients my body was reacting to, but SHAME was the real cause. I was ashamed for what I was feeling, for not being normal like everyone else.

Shame was what fired up my vicious anxiety cycle in this case; otherwise, it would have *just* been nausea. Had I been eating all alone, I would not have felt anxiety, just the nausea.

I'm sure shame is, at least in part, a cause for you too.

Since most people who have followed my coaching over the years never meet me in person, they have a tendency to open up faster, thus helping their recovery. Here are some shame examples of the people I've met over the years:

- The woman who was afraid to hold a knife in the kitchen whenever someone else was present, scared of doing something she had seen in horror movies. The mere thought alone was enough to make her anxious. She would think, "I'm crazy, I must be crazy for having ideas like these!" The more she tried to avoid these thoughts, the more they returned, of course.

  She was not crazy. Everyone has crazy thoughts. Other people are just better at dismissing them, at not caring. The problem was she was too ashamed to talk about these thoughts. Had she done that, she would have found other people who had had them too.

Nevertheless, she was even too ashamed of herself for having these kinds of ideas.

I've met many women and men with this exact same fear who could give the likes of Stephen King a lesson in "coming up with thrilling scenarios." She was not alone.

- The woman who didn't want to be left alone with her baby. She always wanted her husband or mother or anyone else present. She didn't trust herself. This woman believed she would lose her mind or be otherwise unfit to care for her child when left alone.

- The airplane pilot I already talked about who was afraid of flying. Shame was a major cause for him for obvious reasons.

The first step toward his recovery was admitting that he had this ridiculous fear, given his profession. In this case, I was the one he admitted it to, but that was the crucial and necessary step to start his recovery.

- A world famous soccer player who was afraid of getting a panic attack in the middle of the field, with millions of eyes watching his every move. Being a badass soccer player, he was too ashamed to come forward and admit to anyone that this was a fear he had.

- A father who had promised his wife and kids he would finally go on a vacation with them. Weeks before the departure date, his anxiety fiercely increased as he was anticipating getting panic attacks and not being able to return home. He was so afraid to ruin their vacation that he eventually *really* ruined it by cancelling the entire trip beforehand, using the lame excuse of too much going on at work. He was devastated and felt like a failure.

You may start to see a common thread here. Most of these people believed their fears would not be understood by others. They wouldn't *get* it.

At first sight, it seems that shame toward others was at play. Nevertheless, the much deeper lying shame, the shame toward ourselves, is the true cause.

When we, for some reason, can't *own* our flaws and mistakes, we're in fact ashamed of *who* we are. This has a tremendous impact on our self-worth and on our true core confidence.

Anxiety breeds on the gap between the image we want others to have of us, and who we know we really are.

The larger that gap, the bigger the anxiety and the stress you will feel, especially in social situations but not limited to those.

If you want to overcome that shame, you need to recognize it. Shame is a simple fear of being unworthy. Unworthy of love and respect from others when you reveal the real you, flaws included.

First of all, as I'm sure you know, we are all perfectly imperfect. And other people really don't matter as much as we believe they do.

When we show our unique selves to the world, flaws included, and other people freak out, that's their responsibility, not ours. Here too it will be important to let go, to go with the flow and see what happens.

We'll discuss every technique you can use in part two and in the addendum, but I already want to share how I dealt with restaurant situations as I was learning and practicing how to overcome my own anxiety and panic attacks.

I was back in a restaurant, and just like in the good old days the nausea and other symptoms appeared. They never missed a restaurant meal. At first, my anxiety still rose like it used to and I had thoughts like, "Djeezs, why is this happening now? And look, my plate is still SO full. I can't stop eating now! If I do, the waiter is going to ask me what was wrong with it..."

But then I switched tracks.

I changed my thinking to, "Wait, stop. Who cares about the waiter? I am me. If I want to stop eating for ANY reason under the sun, then that's my decision. I have the freedom to decide that. If I throw up and cause a major scene, then I'll deal with it! If I faint, get a red face, or make a fool out of myself in any other way, we may laugh at it during Christmas parties for years to come. Or I may decide to hide under a rock and live there happily ever after, who cares? I'm going with the flow. I'll wait until the nausea subsides, and if it doesn't, I'll stop eating. I probably ate something my body didn't like and that's why I'm nauseous."

Interestingly enough, if I *had* eaten one of the ingredients to avoid, the nausea often stayed, but the anxiety left. In all other cases where it was simply the social restaurant setting that had caused the discomfort, even the nausea dissipated as soon as I was ready to let go *and* not be ashamed about it.

And it did happen that other people asked me, "Is everything all right?" Then I always chose to show my authentic and real self: "Well, my hunger is gone all of a sudden. That's a bit weird. How's your food?"

We need to learn to not make a big deal out of everything and not be ashamed about our uniqueness.

Hereditary?

Some anxious people notice that they are not the only ones in their family that is more anxious than average. It turns out that part of the anxiety can be hereditary. This simply means that your genes might cause you to be more anxious than the general population. If you are an HSP (highly sensitive person), chances are one of your parents had the same trait. First of all, this is not bad news. My father is a man with a lot of anxious tendencies; he loves to worry about the little things, and my grandfather was definitely a very anxious man too. He would get migraine headaches every Sunday just because Monday meant going back to work. So with all that anxiety in my family tree, I must live a life filled with anxiety, right?

Not true. Yes, my predisposition made me walk down the path leading to Panic Ville because it made me more anxious than the average, not-so-anxious Joe. But you can choose to pack your bags and turn back whenever you want. If it were hereditary, I wouldn't have been able to totally overcome my panic attacks more than ten years ago. Your genes are simply a predisposition. A lock. You still decide whether you turn the key or not.

When I look at all of the people I've helped, I believe learned behavior plays a much bigger role. If you had an anxious mother or father while growing up, chances are you've taken over their view of the world.

Did you know for example that babies have no fear of spiders and snakes? Studies show they learn to fear spiders when they hear their mother's reaction to the one that was slowly crawling down the shower curtain one morning.[3]

We have a tendency to take over many of the anxieties of our peers as we are growing up. This, in my opinion, can play a major role and make anxiety seem truly hereditary when it's in fact just learned behavior.

What's the one sentence some parents are repeating over and over again to their children? "Be careful!"

---

[3] Journal of Experimental Child Psychology, Volume 142, February 2016, Pages 382–390

The Nervous System (So Important!)

Your nervous system takes care of just about everything that's going on in your body. From making your mouth water when you're about to indulge in your favorite meal to briskly pulling your hand away when you decided to lean on a sizzling hot stovetop.

There are two major parts to your nervous system, the voluntary and involuntary part.

Every movement you consciously make is part of what the voluntary nervous system takes care of. When you reach for your phone to see how perfect the lives of everyone on social media are, that is your voluntary nervous system at play.

The involuntary nervous system (or the autonomic nervous system), on the other hand, takes care of you without any direct input. Your digestion belongs to this piece of the nervous system. When you eat something, you don't have to focus on your stomach to release exactly one cup of stomach acid and enzymes to break down the burger you just ate. All of that goes on behind the scenes, automatically. Imagine how big our to-do list would get otherwise!

Your heart rate, pupil dilation, and temperature control (sweating or getting goose bumps) are other examples of the involuntary part. We have no *direct* control over it. But your nervous system does! When you're angry, your heart rate goes up (your nervous system asked for it). When you're madly in love, your digestion behaves differently thanks to all of those butterflies taking up space (that's your nervous system again). When your amygdala thinks you're in danger, it tells your nervous system that. In turn, it fires up the entire fight-or-flight response.

Our emotions affect our organs via the involuntary part of the nervous system.

The challenge is that when you misuse it for a long period of time, your nervous system will become so fatigued and worn out that its sensitivity will go up dramatically. It will take less and less to put it in full force and deliver all of the consequences of a bout of anxiety, even though the trigger was something that wouldn't scare other people, not even the 'old you' of a couple of months earlier.

Here's a quick illustration of this process. Imagine that you're swimming in the ocean and you've had to fend off two hungry sharks. They didn't get to bite you because you swim like a dolphin, but they came awfully close and you had to really call them nasty names before they finally decided to turn around. Your nervous system is still stressed because of this encounter and you're quite fatigued considering you've just had to fight for your life, for real this time.

As you're swimming back to shore, you see the fin of a small, elegant, and not at all dangerous baby whale near you. A magical event that would otherwise have made you happy. But now you go into a full state of anxiety exactly because your nervous system became super sensitive. Something *good* just scared you.

The more anxiety or panic attacks you have, the more sensitive the nervous system will become. Even events that should not make you anxious at all can then launch you into a full state of anxiety.

That's why, over time, you might feel that it takes less and less to make you freak out. This is the very reason why the nervous system is a major cause of anxiety. We'll work on calming it down and allowing it to restore itself in part two. Are you ready for it?

Part 2: This Is Where You Get Your Life Back

You now understand what happens during an anxious moment, what the most important causes of anxiety are, and how your nervous system plays a fundamental role. It's time to get your life back and recover.

A little heads up. If you skipped ahead and arrived here without completely reading part one, please go back. Part one is the foundation. You'll need the knowledge I've given you there for part two to work effectively. There are no shortcuts.

The anxiety you have now has forced you to take action. You have reached the "I've had enough of this!" point. Therein lies the gift of becoming a better version of yourself, even better than who you were before your anxiety-related problems started. We'll fight this battle on all fronts, together.

What follows will be built around a couple of pillars.

1. **The mind.** What happens in your mind plays a major role as you've learned. We'll go over how you should talk to yourself when you're anxious and how you can respond to the different types of negative self-talk and "what if?" thinking. This is also where you'll learn how to get your self-esteem back. How to feel safe and sane wherever you are. You don't need a safe place or a safe person. Everything you need is already within you. You'll also learn how to not try to control everything or be a perfectionist. You'll learn how to calm yourself down without outside help from other people, medication, or fleeing to a safer place. You'll learn how to do it then and there, wherever you are.

2. **The body**. You'll learn techniques to calm down your nervous system and you'll learn some of the causes of those weird sensations you might feel. I'll also explain what your body needs to stabilize internally since an unstable body is one that will be sensitive to anxiety and panic attacks.

What follows is your toolbox. Each and every tool will help you swipe some unwanted anxiety off the table. The power comes from using a combination of multiple tools. Try all of them on and see what fits you best. Also see what works best in certain situations (e.g., if you start to feel anxious during a conversation, you won't have a lot of time to go through the more enhanced techniques. That's OK. Simply pick some of the easy and short ones).

It's important to memorize and practice every tool well. The more you practice, the better you will become at it.

The Mind and Your Inner "What If?" Voice

The Skill of Overcoming Anxiety

In order to overcome anxiety, generalized anxiety disorder, panic attacks, phobias, and all related issues, we'll need to create new pathways in the brain.

No worries, this is much easier than it sounds, you've been doing it all your life.

Do you remember that, as you were a toddler, walking was out of the question? How about riding a bike? Do you remember how impossible that seemed? What about using a hammer and a nail for the first time? These may all have been accompanied by pretty painful learning curves.

You've had to consciously put in time and effort to learn how it worked, why it worked and what the rules were. Then after days, weeks, or often months of practicing, you became better and better at it, until at one point it became an automatism. You had created a habit and you could do it without consciously focusing on it.

Something amazing happens when we learn a new skill. Our brain starts to form new neural pathways so that something you first had to consciously focus on can become automated. That's pretty powerful stuff. Now let's use this principle on your anxiety.

If you've suffered from any anxiety-related issue for some time, that anxious or at least negative way of thinking has now become an automatism. That's why you probably seem to get way more negative thoughts than positive ones. For the moment, it's still just a habit of your brain, one that we can change.

Your brain has only so much energy and willpower every day and tries to become as effective and efficient as possible. In order to do so, it cuts corners.

If I tell you I flew from Chicago to L.A. yesterday, your mind will most likely think about airports and airplanes, right? Who says I didn't fly with a helicopter, a hot air balloon, or even a zeppelin? Your mind didn't even consider these options because it would be silly to. When people fly, they most often do it by airplane, so that's the automatic reaction your mind is used to.

Everything we repeat or think often becomes an automatism.

Both the good and the bad repetitions. Your mind makes no distinction!

Nathan Spreng, a neuroscientist at Cornell University, did a scientific meta-analysis on this, together with many other scientists who have been studying the brain for decades.[4]

Whenever you repeat a process, your mind believes it must be important, so it memorizes and automates it. Can you see how essential this is?

Because you repeated being anxious, freaking out, or worrying about everything so often, your mind believes it

---

[4] Functional brain changes following cognitive and motor skills training: a quantitative meta-analysis. (PMID:23093519), Neurorehabilitation and Neural Repair [23 Oct 2012, 27(3):187-199], http://europepmc.org/abstract/MED/23093519

must be very important to you. Why else would you practice it so frequently? It's probably not for fun.

So it strengthens that pathway in your brain, making it easier for you to become anxious... automatically! I was mind blown when I first had this realization.

This, luckily, is reversible because the brain plasticity remains, no matter our age, as other interesting studies prove.[5] And as my clients older than 80 have proven too.

Right now, whenever you have an anxious thought, your mind still habitually goes into the "what if?" mode. We'll just need to reverse that step by step, and this is much easier than you think.

Before we move on, let me prove this both to you and possibly to your negative voice that may be skeptical right now.

Please think of something you do often nowadays, without fear, while it made you anxious at first.

_____

_____

_____

_____

_____

For some people, it's driving their car; for others, it's swimming, riding a bike, horseback riding...

---

[5] https://www.ncbi.nlm.nih.gov/pubmed/17046669, Brain plasticity and functional losses in the aged: scientific bases for a novel intervention.

I still remember the first time I learned how to swim. I was traumatized since, as a toddler, I once stumbled into the kiddy pool and as I was rolling in the water I didn't know where the surface was.

I nearly drowned (so I thought), until my auntie saved me and pulled me up.

Then the first time I hit the big and frighteningly deep pool for a swimming lesson, my heart was beating through my chest as I was super anxious. Not just because of the swimming lesson, I kept waiting for the shark from *Jaws* to surface and eat me alive. But as the lessons progressed and the shark never surfaced, swimming became more and more of an automatism, and my anxiety gradually subsided until it was totally gone.

Have you had similar experiences?

This is the usual way we conquer normal anxiety. By exposing ourselves to it over and over again, we learn that it's OK. The anxiety vanishes, and that scary thing becomes embedded into our comfort circle. We can then partake in it without fear.

Nonetheless, as I'm sure you found out, pure exposure is not enough to conquer *irrational* fears. For those irrational fears, we'll need to take out the heavy toolbox. And that's what part two is for.

Exactly What to Tell Yourself to Overcome Anxiety and Panic Attacks

Your internal dialogue and what you keep telling yourself plays a major role as we've seen. It is what makes the difference between feeling anxious for less than a minute, developing generalized anxiety disorder, having panic attacks, or suffering from phobias.

First, imagine that you're looking after an eight-year-old girl who says, "Hey, I feel scared. I think there's a monster in my closet. I'm afraid."

How will you respond?

Suppose you say, "Oh my! You *should* be afraid! You're right. Even though monsters don't exist, there may be a burglar, a kidnapper or even a serial killer in your closet. And don't get me started about snakes and spiders... And ghosts! Although the jury is still out on those, I believe they exist. Anyway, bad things are about to happen to you either way, my dear. And it's not just your closet you should be afraid of! You have no idea how tough life will get from here on out! Don't you read the newspaper or watch the news? Life is bad. Trust me. I'm an adult. I know everything."

Can you picture the face of the little girl you've been explaining this to? Will this advice help? Of course not! You'll make her cry and scare her even more! That's obvious.

But if this is *so* obvious... the question is, why do anxious people talk in that exact same way to themselves? Their minds go on and on and imagine things that *could* indeed happen, but where the possibility of it actually occurring is less than 1%.

What kinds of things do you say to yourself when you're anxious? I'm sure it's not kind and soothing. You may also be disappointed in yourself just *because* you had the thoughts or the anxiety in the first place. That disappointment is harsh as well.

Imagine lashing out at the eight-year-old girl with, "Why does this always happen to you? Why are you having these fears? I'm so disappointed... " That wouldn't help either.

If you kept track of your self-talk, your inner dialogue, you'd be surprised of how badly you're often treating yourself.

Our internal dialogue during moments of intense anxiety would often be classified as verbal abuse should we use the same language outwardly toward others.

If a real eight-year-old sought your reassurance, I'm sure you would calm the little girl down and say kind things. And that's what you'll need to do with yourself. Self-compassion is crucial!

At every moment of the day while you're awake, you're talking to yourself, all the time. And the road you pick will strongly color your mood, your feelings, your stress level, and of course, your anxiety level.

If you react badly to one negative thought, you'll probably still feel fine. When you keep reacting negatively, you're setting yourself up for constant anxiety.

Here's a common example that I give in my audio course as well:

You're home alone. It's 11 PM, and you're in bed. You hear a sound in your garden that you haven't heard before. Your mind can think, "Oh no, burglars! They probably noticed the courier guy dropping off my new phone and laptop. Heck, it might even BE the courier guy trying to steal it back from me. I *knew* I couldn't trust him! What do I do now? Should I call 911?"

I don't even have to explain how you'll feel if these are the thoughts you choose to believe.

But if your mind would say instead, "That's probably a wild animal trying out some yoga poses and failing miserably at it... or the wind... whatever," you'd feel no fear.

The way you'd feel would be totally different whereas the circumstances (a noise in the yard) would be exactly the same in both cases. The outside world didn't change. The same (bad) thing had happened! But your reaction to it was different, and consequently, your feelings and emotions will differ as well.

You get to decide how you respond to every event that happens in your life.

Anxiety is a choice.

It took me a long time to acknowledge this. How could it possibly be a choice? I didn't *want* the anxiety.

We don't always choose our initial reaction, but we do choose the reaction to that first layer of anxiety. This is called emotional intelligence. We have the power to make an intelligent choice about the thoughts we use and thus the emotions we feel.

I've already mentioned it but want to emphasize it again here. Marcus Aurelius, the great Roman Emperor who lasted two decades as an Emperor (quite a long time when you have that many enemies), wrote in his journal: *"You have power over your mind, not outside events. Realize this, and you will find strength.... If you are distressed by anything external, the pain is not due to the thing itself, but to your estimate of it; and this you have the power to revoke at any moment."*

That's almost twenty centuries ago.

Neurologist and psychiatrist Victor Frankl, the man who not only survived the Nazi death camps but even learned how to have fun while being in the most horrendous place on earth at that time, went on to perfect this.

Let's look at his most famous quote and attitude again from his book *Man's Search for Meaning*, "Everything can be taken from a man but one thing: the last of the human freedoms— to *choose* one's attitude in any given set of circumstances, to choose one's own way."

If you let your thoughts lead the way, you're living your life in a reactive state, and you'll never feel like you are in control.

Easier said than done, of course. I'm sure you have tried to think positive like many gurus always proclaim. But that never works for long or even at all.

So what can you do then when you are minding your own business, and a what-if thought pops up or anything else that makes you anxious?

Step one is to question those negative thoughts.

Counterintuitive questions you can use when you're anxious

Let's look at Jenny first, a client of mine. Jenny is a schoolteacher who feared getting stuck in a traffic jam. Thoughts would pop up, giving her claustrophobic anxiety. As she listened to and agreed with her thoughts, her anxiety would get stronger and stronger, eventually giving her a panic attack. She was simply following the vicious cycle model I explained earlier on.

In order to avoid these anxious sensations, Jenny started to take long detours and did everything she could to dodge traffic jams. That, of course, was not a solution. It's a pure catch-22. The more you run away from anxiety, the more it will find you. In this case, her averting traffic jams was confirming to her body and mind that they were indeed dangerous.

I explained to Jenny that as long as she was giving power and attention to those negative thoughts, as long as she feared them, they would have tremendous authority over her. It took me a while to convince Jenny because at first she didn't see it that way. "I don't have a choice, Geert," she said "That anxiety and those thoughts just come, and there's nothing I can do about it."

"Sure," I explained to her, "and as long as you believe *that* you are right. On the other hand, when you decide to look at it from another perspective, as hard as that may seem, you'll get more power."

"You are still launching the vicious panic attack cycle by thinking the way you currently think, by simply following the anxious thoughts, by considering them as the one and only truth. Next time, try to question them. These thoughts do not originate from an all-knowing oracle that is always right. They are just thoughts. Try to verify their validity by openly questioning them."

Jenny started to work on this, which was very hard for her at first. Her mind had been automatically going into the anxiety direction for a long time. It was challenging to switch channels. But as she kept repeating to herself, "Is that really true? Am I REALLY in a life-or-death situation by being in this traffic jam? Is <u>certain</u> death as imminent as my thoughts want me to believe?"

At first, her mind came back with, "Yes! I am about to die. This is dangerous!" Then Jenny countered with, "Is that really, really true?" This could go on for a while, until one thought finally popped into her head, "No, that's not true. It's not *that* bad. There is no imminent danger."

This thought surprised Jenny, as she later explained to me. It was the first positive idea that allowed her to question her other anxious thoughts more easily. She now knew her thoughts were not always valid. One minute they tried to convince her she had to get out of there, the next they confirmed it was not that bad. Hmm...

Jenny learned how to overcome her anxiety and panic attacks together with the other techniques in this book. Her anxious thoughts were simply warning her for things that would probably never happen, and yet she had been considering them as the only possible outcome for years.

As you've seen, by continuously questioning those negative thoughts she had prior, she started to create a new pathway in her thinking that became more and more automated.

That muscle became stronger and stronger. Questioning these thoughts had exposed how faulty and misleading her original anxious thoughts often were. They were just playing a mind game!

This is a hard and an important first step. I've personally helped hundreds of people to make the switch and seen thousands do it through the audio program I have on my website. So you can do this too, no matter what your negative thoughts are about.

Thinking in a non-anxious way is like picking up the heavy weights in the gym you cannot lift yet. How do you get to a point where you can lift them up with relative ease? You start with lighter weights, you train, and you allow the muscle to grow and become stronger.

That's what you'll need to do with your mind as well. Train it, and it will become stronger!

As a first step, I would like to ask you to question your own negative thoughts whenever you have them. Whenever something scares you and gives you the anxiety you're trying to leave behind, analyze what you had just been thinking. Observe what your mind comes up with.

What was the first domino? What thought led you to having the anxiety? What thought triggered it?

Please realize it will have been a thought. It's not the location, the thing you saw, the sensation you felt, or the people you're with that gave you the anxiety. It will have been a thought that you had as a reaction to what happened. What was your thought? Write it down as soon as you can afterward.

When you have good anxiety, like the anxiety you'll feel when you see a tarantula bathing itself in your bathtub, it will be caused by an instinctive reaction led by your amygdala, the part of your brain that instantly decides whether something is a threat or not.

With bad anxiety, it will most often be a thought that starts with, "Oh no, what if?" or "What will people think if?" or "What's this symptom I'm feeling?" etc.

Jenny did not have fears because of the traffic jam she was in. The traffic jam was never at fault; it represented no real danger. It was the thought that popped up and said, "I can't get away now. I'm stuck, so what if..." that caused everything in her case.

For the next couple of days I would like you to look for your trigger thoughts. What are they? What makes the first domino drop?

It often goes like this:

- You see something > thought and anxiety trigger > anxiety
- You feel something > thought and anxiety trigger > anxiety
- You see someone > thought and anxiety trigger > anxiety

I admit there are exceptions to this rule. It can happen that you've had a serious bout of anxiety in a certain location and being in the same or a similar place gives you the initial feeling of anxiety. That's because your mind remembered how seemingly life threatening your previous experience was and wants you to avoid it.

Every time we panic like a maniac or act like a bloodthirsty tiger has just started to lick our legs, our brain remembers the exact setting this horrendous event took place in. It will do everything it can to have you avoid it the next time.

Thinking about it will be enough to launch all of the symptoms. But even then, they are still thoughts that will raise the anxiety level and potentially start the vicious cycle.

For the next couple of days, please write down your trigger thoughts. The ones you've had right before the anxiety rose significantly.

As soon as you have pinpointed your trigger thoughts, question them. Ask questions like "Is it really *that* bad?" and "Is this really *that* life threatening that I have to respond as if I'm surrounded by hungry tigers who have been fed a vegan diet for months?" and "Am I really in trouble?" and "Do I really have a problem, right now, in this present moment?"

Question their validity. Question whether the anxiety system that had been launched was really needed to come to a solution. It wasn't if you weren't in any real, imminent, physical danger.

Questioning negative thoughts takes away their power, as you'll start to discover.

But this is only the beginning of what we can do, so here is another technique.

Choosing what thoughts to weigh in on

Imagine a flood of thoughts passing through your head, like a little river of ideas and concepts you think of. If you don't pay attention to a thought, it will just pass and be gone. If, on the other hand, you do place importance on a thought, you take it aside and will feel its full power (positive or negative).

What thoughts are you currently taking aside?

Let me give you an example. Here is a set of thoughts that could pass through your head at any given time:

"I wonder what the weather will be like tomorrow. The movie I saw yesterday was great. Shouldn't forget to pick up my dry cleaning after work. Do I still have some bananas at home? I'd like to make a milkshake. What will I cook for dinner tonight? Something light, I have an important meeting tomorrow. Did Rachel text me back yet about that birthday gift we're buying for Monica?"

In this example, you simply let the train of thoughts pass and nothing happens to your emotions. There is no anxiety.

What you could have done instead was put more importance on a certain thought and launch the anxiety cycle. Here's an example:

"... Do I still have some bananas at home? I want to make a milkshake. What will I cook for dinner tonight? Something light, I have an important meeting tomorrow. Oh no! That meeting is tomorrow already? What if I don't sleep well? What if I start to tremble as I hand out the slides and my colleagues see it? And I hope the traffic won't be too bad. Last time I drove, I felt bad. Oh and I'll probably start to sweat during that meeting, God. I forgot to wash that one shirt I have that hides the waterfalls my armpits turn on whenever I'm presenting. Oh no, it's going to be a disaster. And my boss may even fire me when my next review comes by, just like he did with Casey."

Do you see what happened here? At first you had a simple stream of thoughts and you didn't pay any additional attention to one thought in particular. They just passed by without changing your emotions. The first train of thoughts had no power over you since you didn't *give* them any power.

In the second example, however, you took one thought apart and gave it power. This exact thought is the first bad domino that starts a flood of negative thoughts, leading to the catastrophe of a job loss. Not long after you start to weigh in on this thought, more mind games come into play.

If you suffer from any form of anxiety, this probably sounds familiar. The first domino is the most important one. That's the moment you'll have to start using the techniques I'm explaining now, like questioning the validity of that negative thought.

Here are some examples of questions that will direct your mind away from anxiety in this particular example:

"Really? Am I REALLY going to lose my job if I don't sleep well tonight? Do I really need to worry *that* much about this? Is it worth it that I get all of this anxiety and that my day today will be ruined because of that meeting tomorrow? Even if it's an important one? Will I die as a result of having a bad meeting tomorrow? Will the sun stop coming up in the morning?"

Questioning a negative thought works well. Using humor works even better in some cases.

Humor

Anxiety and humor are opposites. If you get chased by a real-life tiger, it will be impossible to laugh or have fun in any way. So having fun, when you're anxious, communicates a very strong message to your entire anxiety system, "NO, I'm not being chased by a real tiger. This is a false alarm."

Let's get back to our previous example with the passing thought stream. What if you would respond like this:

"... something light, I have an important meeting tomorrow. Oh no! That meeting is tomorrow already. Yep, it is... And I could now start to freak out like the neurotic Ross from the TV sitcom *Friends*, but that won't help. Besides, I'm so ridiculous. I tend to panic about the little things as if I'm being chased by tigers all the time." With this kind of reasoning, you're exposing that negative thought for what it is: FEAR (false evidence appearing real).

When I had my light-headedness I would for instance think, "Other people need to drink alcohol to feel dizzy like this. I can just switch it on without booze! Cool."

This sounds childish, but the anxious thought stream you would normally be having will be as well anyway.

Even a silly, "Right, here I go again. If freaking out over nothing ever becomes an Olympic sport, I'm sure I could win a medal!"

It really doesn't matter what you think or choose, as long as you take away the power of that first domino. Laugh with it or do the opposite of what your body expects.

Do the opposite: "Bring it on! I want to cuddle!"

This creates a small short-circuit in your brain that will say, "Wait what?" That's often all you need to create an opening and get the necessary altitude to realize it's just a false alarm.

As explained, it is crucial not to fear the fear. This technique will help you do that. But it is designed to do even more.

First, we need to remember that when the anxiety system launches and we're not in real, actual, imminent danger, it is misfiring. Anxiety serves no other purpose than helping you when you're in an *imminent* life-or-death situation.

You may know rationally that there is no danger, but you will oftentimes find that the body doesn't follow right away. That's because your amygdala and other systems are still convinced there *is* a threat. A real one.

What we'll need to do here is create a disconnect in your mind. One of the many ways to do this is to firmly state, "Sure, whatever. BRING IT ON! Come on, I'm ready to cuddle!"

That's the last thing your body and the famous alarm system will be expecting.

Let's take a step back and look at an example. Kelly is sitting in a hot meeting room with musty air, surrounded by slick, straight-faced colleagues with ties and one even with a bow tie. As it's almost her time to speak, she gets a whole range of bodily sensations that make her want to run out and never return. That, evidently, wouldn't be good for her career. And the thought of that makes her anxiety even worse! She feels trapped and breaks out in a sweat.

Kelly's usual reaction would be to try and manage this anxiety as much as she could and, if needed, excuse herself and run off to the restrooms.

This time, however, she does the opposite. Here's her thought train: "My gosh, I'm sweating like a pig. I'm sure my colleagues can see it. What if... Hold it! Stop. You know what, bring it on! I don't care. Show me what you've got, make it worse, make me feel bad, make it as bad as it can get. I'm ready, bring it on! Turn me into a sweaty pig! I want to find out if all of the bad consequences I keep imagining will *really* happen or not. I'm ready. I'm done fighting, so bring it on!"

Just as your mind may now say, "Wait what?" so will her body, her amygdala, and *her* mind! It's the opposite of what it expects. Here they are—her body, amygdala, and so forth—preparing for an imminent attack by angry tigers with bow ties, and she demands *more* of it? What? Disconnect.

This very technique may be all that's needed to subside the unwanted anxiety. It proves to your body that there is indeed no real danger, for if that were to be the case, there's no way a sane person like yourself would ever demand more or run toward the problem. So the fact that you *do* must mean that the fire alarm is misfiring. Your body then calms down and turns it off.

This may take a couple of minutes, but running or managing the anxiety will not be needed. It will leave because you will be turning it off. Nevertheless, there are of course more techniques you can deploy, should they be needed.

One of the most powerful ways to respond to anxiety is to just let go and go with the flow. Here's my magical sentence I've been explaining to my clients for over a decade:

"Whatever happens, it's OK."

This is *the* strongest antidote to any type of anxiety you will EVER see and get.

Truth be told, it will be one you'll have to practice since it is hard to apply at first. That's normal. Just like learning how to swim or ride a bike, persistent practice is all it takes. Bear with me while I give you a freaky example.

Imagine a guy, wearing a gray suit, standing in an elevator of an office building. All of a sudden, he feels a sharp pain in his chest and numbness in his left arm. His mind thinks, "God no! I'm having a heart attack." As a result, he gets a jolt of anxiety, the adrenaline rush. However, instead of going down the vicious anxiety and panic cycle, he says, "SO? So what? If this is my time to die, so be it, I'm ready."

Let's forgo the fact whether or not it would be absolutely ridiculous to have such thoughts for now. The question is: do you think he will still feel anxiety? No. He totally dismissed the anxious thought and has wiped it off the table. His adrenaline level will soon get back to a normal level even though his physical symptoms may still be present for a while.

Your mind will now probably wonder, "Sure, Geert. Sounds great, but what if he's having a REAL heart attack? Then what? How does he know the difference? What if... " Good question! I knew your what-if engine was waiting to jump into action. The force is strong in you, as expected.

He doesn't know, and it doesn't matter, anxiety-wise.

The real question is: does anxiety serve him? If it doesn't, it is not needed. If he's really having a heart attack, the additional anxiety won't help him. It will probably make everything worse. So it actually doesn't matter. What he could do, should he wish, is add, "If the pain persists, I'll call an ambulance, but I choose not to fear what I'm feeling now. Whatever happens, it's OK. I'll deal with it when it gets worse, and for now, I'll let my heart beat however hard or slow it wants to."

I get that this new way of thinking is going to give you a lot of mental resistance. That's OK. Your mind is still wired to be anxious at this time.

Let's notice that the sentence says "OK," not "fun, nice, cool, not bad." OK is about acceptance, about not letting in additional anxiety. That's it.

"Whatever happens, it's OK" is so powerful because even though the worst outcome might be one of the possibilities, it won't happen in 99.9% of the real-life outcomes. So why flood your entire life with anxiety and unhappiness for something that will, realistically, probably not even happen...

Now even then, I found time and time again that the true power toward anxiety lies in accepting *even* that worst possible outcome and deciding to be OK with it.

That's hard, I admit. It even may seem impossible for you at this point. That too, is normal.

This was a very important personal choice I've had to make in the past. I didn't want the anxiety to control my life any longer, so **I accepted the "whatever happens, it's OK,"** *even* **in situations where the worst possible outcome would obviously not be OK.**

Whereas my previous habit had been constantly playing the what-if game with anxiety as a consequence, I now, after many weeks of practicing, had a new habit of immediately letting go of control and just going with the flow, even if that flow would bring me somewhere I would opt to avoid.

Although I never preferred the "what ifs" to become reality, I refrained from trying to control *everything,* and I let go, right away.

That trying-to-control approach is what I had been practicing for fourteen years, and it worked abominably with not only zero results but even a severe increase in the way anxiety dominated my life.

I explain the "whatever happens" mentality all throughout this book because I want you to have a 360° view of its powerful impact on your negative emotions. We'll also keep going over ways you can implement it. The addendum at the very end will then give you means to use it in specific situations and with certain symptoms.

In short, here is how it works:

"What if this bad thing happens to me?" > "SO? So what? Whatever! I don't give a darn anymore, been there done that. Whatever happens, it's OK." > No anxiety. It's that simple.

I remember one of the last overseas flights I took. There was serious turbulence, the kind where the overhead cabinets fall open and even the crew seems worried. I'm not a robot; I'm a human being so I immediately started to worry and wonder if I was going to die.

My old programming, the old automatic response of my mind, would have taken that "I'm going to die" thought, get super scared, put a lot of weight on it, start to freak out, planned my exit, and would have made me feel super bad until the turbulence stopped. And even then I would have felt shaken up for a long time after. Heck, I might have decided to never fly again based on that experience alone and done all of my travelling by boat.

Is that silly in your opinion? Would it be silly to be so scared of flying based on that one moment of strong turbulence? It *is* silly, isn't it?

Please keep that in mind. My overanxious reaction was silly. Turbulence is a normal side effect of flying. It's complementary.

So I've trained my mind to follow another silly route, the one without anxiety. It happened automatically during the turbulence but please remember that I've had to train this. It only became an automatism because I had been consciously working on mastering it for a couple of months, back in 2004. Here was my actual train of thoughts:

"Yup, Geert, this is it! A plane cannot withstand this. The wings won't be able to hold. You're probably going to crash and die right now!" (This is my first unstoppable anxious thought stream, I could not have prevented it. But now I take over.) "Yup, that's it, Geert. Your life is indeed over. That's OK though! You know how you love to watch *Airplane Investigation* on Natural Geographic, well, you'll finally be *in* it! They may even make a movie of what's about to happen. Isn't that great. So come on, enjoy the ride. YIHAAA!"

I sat there with a smile, actually enjoying the turbulence as if it was an amusement park ride while most of the other people were scared.

You may be thinking that what I just said is ridiculous, even totally stupid. I agree, it is! Thinking like that is really silly, childish even. Remember, however, that thinking you're going to die is silly as well; we came to that conclusion in a previous paragraph. So I chose the path of silliness with no anxiety.

Just imagine that each and every time you've had a panic attack or any moment of unwanted anxiety in the past year, it had been replaced by a moment of silliness and fun. *How much fun would you be having?* A lot, I guess.

You survived each and every moment of anxiety you've had, otherwise you wouldn't be reading this now, *even* though your mind told you your life was over, your dignity was about to be smashed, or some other apocalypse would happen to you. You're still here. The sun still comes up every morning. So it *was* silly to be anxious at those times. Why not use the second path of silliness then if it means the anxiety will fall away?

Please take as much time as you need to let this sink in. I understand your mind will be resisting what I've just described. This is normal.

I know anxiety is not fun, the sensations are no fun and I'm in no way trying to downplay how uncomfortable it is... but worrying about it, following the vicious cycle, and making everything worse is what you've been practicing for a while. And it didn't work! Otherwise, you wouldn't be reading this book; my jokes just aren't funny enough.

So, we'll throw the old way of thinking overboard and try something new. I hope you're with me and are ready to give it a try. *This* is the key.

No, it's not really OK!

Some people who followed the first edition of my audio course often wrote me an e-mail stating, "Sure, Geert. 'Whatever happens, it's OK' would work if I'm afraid to, for example, sweat in front of other people. But no, I'm afraid that I will die or that really bad things will happen to me. THEY ARE NOT OK!"

Of course they are not! I prefer not to be on National Geographic as an airplane crash victim you know... It's just a simple *choice* I make. The anxiety doesn't serve me during turbulence. I'm not the pilot, and I haven't brought a parachute as my one carry-on item. I can't do anything about the predicament I'm in, so I might as well give myself over to whatever will happen. And this of course doesn't just apply to airplanes and turbulence.

That said, I totally understand the internal resistance you may feel now. I had it too.

Most anxiety is created by mind games like catastrophizing. Your mind believes the absolute worst *is* going to happen. But it has no proof... Here is where *we* start to play a game ourselves. If the negative voice tries to scare you, fine. Instead of going down this negative path, say, "Sure! Bring it on! Whatever happens, it's OK" and make it sound ridiculous. All of the *bad* anxiety you've felt that made you reach for this book had no use! There was no real and imminent life-or-death danger (if there were, it would have been *good* anxiety).

Total acceptance is the key. But you will have to mean it. It's pointless to feel anxious and then say, "Whatever happens, it's OK. Bring it on" in hopes of making your anxiety go away. Here, you'd still fear the fear, and that would be feeding the anxiety.

This is a concept that the late Dr. Claire Weekes spent a lot of time researching as well. As long as there is no total acceptance, the nervous system will remain under too much pressure and the anxiety will continue to flourish.

I can tell you from personal experience that this is hard! Very hard! Nevertheless, it is the key.

You have a choice.

Please make the "whatever happens it's OK, and I mean it" choice for the next couple of weeks. Invite the anxiety and all of its entourage of sensations in when it comes knocking at your door. For if you don't, if you try to run, slam the door shut or pretend it isn't there, it will tear down the walls of your house. Then, only then, does anxiety become a true beast, one with the power to destroy the quality of our lives.

Why is that?

Because all your anxiety wants is to be acknowledged. It wants some love, some attention, and even some recognition for all it does for you. For as we've seen, anxiety *does* save your life every single day. It points out the true and real dangers as well and we owe it not to fear it, if only for that.

Unwanted anxiety is just a feeling, a sensation, a misguided fire alarm. The "what if?" thoughts you are getting are not real, you're not in any real danger, for if you really were, it wouldn't be unwanted anxiety in the first place. If you don't see a clear and *present* danger, it *is* unwanted anxiety.

Constant negative news is OK.

Whatever is causing your anxiety (symptoms, a location, an upcoming event) doesn't really matter because it will only give you the baseline level of anxiety. Your thoughts will create the rest of the turmoil.

I call those thoughts the little cartoonish Donald Duck Devil or the negative radio station.

We all have this negative radio, and people like us, prone to anxiety, have a very well-developed antenna that picks up on everything.

A lot of people despise those thoughts and don't want to have them. They tell me: "I want to be normal. I want to stop my negative thoughts altogether." Well, again, you have a better chance of single-handedly ending world hunger than accomplishing this.

These negative thoughts will need to be accepted too. They are OK. But we will be able to reduce them, just and especially not by trying to have less negative thoughts... as counterintuitive as that will sound.

As I told many of the people who have followed my audio course throughout the years, "Learn to love the fact that your mind is so inventive. That it has the power to come up with so many scenarios and compliment your unlimited creativity for scaring you in new ways. The best horror and thriller writers in Hollywood could learn a lesson or two from your mind's creativity."

The smarter and more creative you are, the sillier and more ridiculous the types of thoughts you will get (on top of all of your genius insights). You can't *just* have good, creative ideas. Your mind will always go in all directions.

When your mind comes up with what ifs, congratulate it. Say, "Wow, what else you've got?" and admire it.

Observe it.

This is important. Take a step back, and look at that fountain of negativity.

Because then you will start to see it for what it really is: Your personal radar, trying to keep you safe, trying to warn you for the real dangers like snakes, and the most ridiculous fake 'dangers' like passing out in the supermarket, losing your mind, making a fool of yourself, or whatever else it comes up with in your case.

These are just the mind games that I'll discuss in more detail in the addendum. We can't stop them. You will always have negative sensations (symptoms) and negative thoughts. You're not a robot. So we have two options:

1. Fear them. That's what you've been doing all this time. I guess we can conclude this option doesn't work out very well.

2. Admire them, have fun with them, see how great they are at dishing up the most remarkable and ridiculous chain of events.

Option two always wins. The more you play with your anxiety, the more you befriend it, the better the quality of your life will be *and* the calmer your danger radar will eventually get.

Let me emphasize this: option two helps you to have a less sensitive danger radar, eventually giving you less and less unwanted anxiety for dangers that are not real and of course, less negative thoughts.

But if you always jump upon everything your radar serves you as a possible threat, your amygdala (that part of your brain that sets in motion your anxiety system) will grow so much and your nervous system will tire so much that your danger radar will become more and more sensitive, making you much more susceptible to even more anxiety.

A 2013 Stanford University study does show indeed that our amygdala will grow and become stronger (thus creating more anxiety) the more anxious and stressed we are.[6]

Why wouldn't it?

If you're truly attacked by tigers every single day, it *is* important to always be on guard and never relaxed. Yet even

[6] https://med.stanford.edu/news/all-news/2013/11/size-connectivity-of-brain-region-linked-to-anxiety-level-in-young-children-study-shows.html

antelopes in the wild savannah don't have to fear attacks every single day.

Much of what you're learning here will also assist in reversing this. And later on in the book, you'll even get a scientifically proven technique to reduce the size of your amygdala. The good news is it can indeed shrink as well, the less it is used, as a study shows.[7]

As you try this new approach, at first, your radar will still be sensitive. Certain thoughts and situations will effortlessly give you that jolt of adrenaline and that will make you anxious.

Please, remember that adding additional anxiety always is a choice, no matter at what point of the vicious cycle you are located at that moment. Even if you have already gotten that first electric jolt, the racing heart, crazy thoughts, and the pit in your stomach, you can *still choose* to say, "Hold on! Wow, danger radio, you had me going here. Thanks for being there, but I'm not going to tune into you right now. If you want to stay, fine, I'll just take you with me then."

You're a grown-up. You're a smart person, and you're definitely no longer a nine-year-old child. But your anxiety system *is!* It is primitive, as we've seen. So it is important to have this soothing self-talk as if you would be talking to an anxious child.

[7] Stress reduction correlates with structural changes in the amygdala, Soc Cogn Affect Neurosci. 2010 Mar; 5(1): 11–17.
https://www.ncbi.nlm.nih.gov/pmc/articles/PMC2840837/
Published online 2009 Sep 23. doi: https://dx.doi.org/10.1093%2Fscan%2Fnsp034, https://www.ncbi.nlm.nih.gov/pmc/articles/PMC2840837/

Calling Out the Name

Another technique against anxiety that I want to throw in the mix is "observing." This is especially helpful when a feeling or a symptom that you desperately try to avoid launches your anxiety. You may sense that sensation often or, on the other hand, it may take a leave of absence only to return with vengeance (just when you thought you were freed of it).

These sensations will often be a simple reaction of your body to something (an ingredient, a smell, something toxic/chemical, an upcoming change, something you've been stressing about for a while).

You've gotten a tremendous amount of insights and knowledge throughout this book. Use it to observe what's happening when you feel something strange. You'll frequently be able to explain *why* you're feeling what you're feeling based on what you've learned here.

Like you, I'm not a robot either, so it can happen that I have a strange sensation that I dislike. Here's how I personally respond to those using the "calling out the name" method:

- Vertigo, dizziness, moment of feeling weak, nausea, "OK, I probably ate or smelled something that my body doesn't like at all, and it's now reacting to that. That's fine. Glad to see my defense system still works."

- Vertigo, dizziness, and moments of nausea in a very populated social setting: "OK, my body is picking up on the fact that there is less oxygen here than outdoors. It's now launching the fight-or-flight system because it wants me to get out of here. It's wrong. I'm not in any danger. I'm not in a cave or a coal mine where oxygen will actually deplete. I'm staying. Oh and yes, should I now faint, vomit, or make a fool out of myself in any other way, then I totally accept that too, bring it on!" This is one I've had to use often, because I have a very sensitive "low oxygen" alarm in my body. But since I no longer run for safety, those sensations go away after a couple of minutes.

- Pounding heart/rapid heartbeat: "I probably ate something I'm allergic to or my body's fighting with a virus. Glad to see my immune system is still functioning. Keep it up!"

So what I do is that I calmly explain some of the possibilities with thoughts other than "You're about to die!" or "People will start to reject me soon because of this."

I simply observe and choose to not freak out. Plus, when I can, I add a little layer of ridiculous humor, just to play with my negative voice.

But the most important aspect of this technique remains the observing, going over why we may be feeling it. This technique of observing can also be powerful for other reasons as well. It has an effect on our amygdala.

Whenever you have a panic attack or serious bout of anxiety, your amygdala is at play. It has then decided something is a danger and instantly raised the threat level. Sometimes even without you having an anxious thought first.

We've already seen that it will deliberately misjudge situations and give you anxiety when none was needed! It has to. When something has even a hint of danger, your amygdala will classify it as danger and push the alarm button. Better safe than sorry indeed.

There is a way to deal with this. A 2007 study done at UCLA by psychologist Matthew Lieberman has shown that calling out the emotion you are feeling can instantly calm down the amygdala.

This means that a simple "Hey, I'm feeling anxious. It's just anxiety" has the power to calm you down.

Whatever set of techniques you decide to use from this book, make sure to include this one. If you feel an unwanted emotion, any emotion, call it out, explain why you feel it. This will help you calm that emotion down, silly as this technique may sound.

When your amygdala makes a call, your reaction to it proves it right or wrong.

If you faced a real, hungry tiger and your amygdala launched the fight-or-flight response, you'd run as if your life depended on it... because it would. If, however, you were walking around in the woods on a Sunday afternoon and heard a sudden movement behind you, your amygdala would raise the anxiety instantly as you turned around and looked for the danger. When you then saw it was a cute little rabbit, your inner dialogue would say, "Oh, it's just a rabbit." Thus, this thought would calm down your amygdala. That's why we've been spending so much time on your inner dialogue throughout this book. When you feel anxious, whatever you say to yourself next will matter a lot.

Calling out the emotion you are feeling and explaining what's happening is powerful. This is a great example of emotional intelligence at play. Use the knowledge you have, from now on, and explain to yourself what's happening and why it's happening.

Pushing anxiety over the edge

Humor is the antidote to anxiety, as I've already briefly discussed.

Anxiety simply cannot survive in the presence of humor. There are multiple ways for you to use humor whenever you are anxious, on top of those already discussed earlier on in the book. Here are some more:

Exaggeration

If your negative voice isn't yet doing it on its own, it can help to push your anxious thoughts into the realm of total ridiculousness.

Cara, one of my clients, was afraid of what other people would think of her when her face flushed all red. This regularly happened when she saw someone she knew at a random place like the supermarket, when she had an important talk at work, and in other circumstances where she was surprised to see someone she deemed important.

Cara told me she then had thoughts like, "I hope I don't get a red face. I'm blushing. I can feel it. I've got to get away from here, or people will think I'm weak and ridiculous, or worse, they'll ask me why I'm blushing and then I won't know what to say."

So I asked Cara to exaggerate the next time and to push her thoughts over the edge. I asked her to turn her thoughts into, "Oh my God. What if I get as red as a lobster? Or a tomato? What if I get so red that people wonder if I'm a cartoon version of the devil himself? And what if they say, 'Cara, you're so weak I can't even continue to talk to you. I hate you!' What if an online group would be created called 'Red Cara' and that group gets thousands of fans?" As you can see, we were slightly exaggerating here.

Cara diligently gave this a try the next time and sent me an e-mail reporting what had happened: as she was pushing herself over the edge, she had started to laugh, with and at herself. She realized how totally ridiculous her thoughts were and as a result, there was a disconnect from the anxiety.

The man she was talking to asked her why she laughed, and she responded, "Oh nothing, don't worry I just thought of something funny I heard. So tell me, how are the kids?" And she continued the conversation.

This can be a powerful technique for two reasons:

1. It uses humor, the antidote to anxiety.
2. It instantly demonstrates that you have no fear of the fear.

Since you dare to push your anxious thoughts even further, you're clearly proving to yourself you don't fear them. This is super powerful.

Ben, another client, was a hypochondriac. He had several weird sensations in his body that scared him all the time. He visited many doctors, trying to get a diagnosis that never came. He had thoughts like: "I sense my heart just skipped a beat, I'm going to die and my life will be over. And oh no, I still want to see my daughter graduate high school. How will my wife then make enough money to support herself and the children?" A couple of days later, he noticed a strange color on his skin, convincing him that he had skin cancer. His train of negative, anxious thoughts often led him to get a panic attack on top of the generalized anxiety disorder he was living with. Not fun, as you can imagine.

So I asked Ben to use the same technique. I explained to him that I often call this technique the "According to Jim" technique. I don't know if you have ever seen that old TV show, but Jim, played by Jim Belushi, plays a stereotyped dad married to his stereotyped wife Cheryl. Cheryl always worries about everything. Jim, on the other hand, often doesn't worry about anything at all as real men supposedly do. Funny, since my client base is almost equally filled with women and men. In a certain episode, Cheryl starts the "what if?" train and launches some worries, to which Jim loudly replies, "What if? What if this? What if that? What if a cat gives birth to a dog?" That silly moment in that TV show helped me develop this technique.

Here too, I asked Ben to push his negative thoughts over the edge. He asked me for an example, so I told him:

The next time you think, "What if I'm having a heart attack?" simply add, "Yeah, what if my heart will start to beat out of my chest like I've seen in cartoons? What if I die here, right now and it turns out the TV show *The Walking Dead* was real and I wake up as a zombie? Or what if the ambulance comes to get me and as they are driving me to the hospital they get into a terrible accident? And as the ambulance crashes the doors fly wide open and I get pushed out on the highway. What if five cars, one bus, and a semi-truck consecutively run over me while recording it with their dash cams? What if that video then goes viral on the Internet and my daughter has to see it? What if they play that video on the big screen during her graduation? And what if my daughter then starts to laugh and says, 'I never loved my dad anyway. Look at what a loser and nitwit he is. He can't even die properly...'"

Ben actually took notes and followed this script to the letter the next time he had a panic attack caused by his heart pounding fast.

As he gave me feedback afterward, he had the same reaction Cara had. The first couple of exaggerations slightly increased his anxiety, but as it came into the ridiculous zone he started to laugh as he continued to read the script out loud.

Again, the disconnect took place, and he realized his thoughts were as ridiculous as the script. They were not based upon reality. And hey, even if they were, "whatever happens, it's OK. I'll see it when it happens." The power never lies in one technique alone but in a combination of what works well for you. This technique not only works well with anxiety; you can apply it on other simple worries as well. Push them over the edge and start exaggerating for fun. This will make it much easier to see how ridiculous some of your negative thoughts and worries are.

If you'd like to try this technique to see what it can do for you, there are two ways to go about this.

1. Do it on the spot. Your anxiety voice, the little cartoon devil, will start to talk and will make you scared. Here you simply join the conversation with, "Yeah, but you know what, what if..." and then you make it all worse, <u>a lot worse!</u> You must arrive in the realm of ridiculousness as you've seen with Ben and Cara.

2. If you find out option one is too hard because you're not able to think clearly on the spot, that's OK. You

may be in a conversation or in the midst of having a panic attack at that time. Write down or record your anxious thoughts immediately afterward. So note the exact phrases your negative voice came up with, word by word. Then, when the wave of anxiety has totally passed, take a piece of paper and push the anxious thoughts over the edge, on paper. Write your exaggerations down, just like I did for Ben. Then keep that piece of paper with you, or put it in your phone.

The next time your mind starts to worry about something similar, take the script you've just created, start reading those exaggerations, and add them to the discussion your negative voice is having in order to simply push it over the top.

Please try this technique multiple times. It's a really powerful one, and I find it helps most, not to say all people who gave it a try.

The fact of pushing your anxious thoughts over the edge will be scary because you're probably trying to not have those negative thoughts at all.

How well has that been working for you?

Here we're doing the opposite, we're demanding more and more. This proves you don't fear the fear anymore, which is very important, and will push it into the zone of humor, which is the antidote to anxiety.

The "Let's Do This" Technique

The "let's do this" technique is a powerful technique to overcome anxiety, especially when it's a fear that is truly not real. This technique is a very strong form of exposure, often called flooding.

It works really well for:

- Fearing that you are going to lose your mind and go crazy
- Fearing that something bad will happen to you in a certain location that other people don't fear at all
- Having a fear of flying, heights, social interactions, etc.

Exposure is a great way to decrease and overcome some forms of anxiety naturally. Everything you now take for granted (walking, swimming, bicycle riding) was once very scary. But you exposed yourself to it at a young age and kept at it until the anxiety dissipated. It always does!

"Not true," say some of my clients at first. "I've been doing the thing I fear for years, but my fear is still here!" They then give me examples like using public transportation while going to work, having a social phobia but still attending meetings, having a fear of driving/flying but still doing it—with fear— since it's a professional obligation and so on.

And my clients are of course right, they have been exposing themselves to what it is they fear and the anxiety did stay. There is a clear and simple explanation for it.

If pure exposure—simply exposing yourself to what it is you fear—were enough, it would be fairly easy to overcome anxiety. Most of the therapists and psychiatrists I talked to when I still had agoraphobia were trying that technique on me too, and it never worked.

Let's look for the difference.

Why does a kid learning to ride a bike eventually get over the fears he feels? What's different compared to an adult trying to overcome his fear of driving while still taking the car to drop the kids off at school, and then quickly returning home?

The distinction lies in the mindset.

The kid thinks, "Let's do this! I want to learn to ride my bike so I can go places and have fun with my friends!"

The adult thinks, "My gosh, I'm so afraid to drop the kids off at school with the car. Let me quickly take the car, swallow the pain, and get it over with as quickly as I can. I hope there won't be too much traffic."

The mindset is totally different. The kid knows the anxiety is just a side effect, and that it will eventually pass, and to be honest, **the kid just doesn't care about the anxiety. He takes it with him and does it anyway**.

The adult, on the other hand, fears the anxiety. He wants to manage and control it as well as he can, but he dreads it. For every second of the activity, the adult will be fighting the anxiety, wishing it weren't there and hoping that it will all be over quickly.

Where the adult tries to avoid the anxiety, the kid *wants* to feel the fear; he wants to ride his bike. He knows the fear comes with it. It's his intention to feel the fear and overcome it.

Can you sense the distinction?

Chances are that whenever you are faced with anxiety or the panic attacks you have, you try to control them, manage them, avoid them, or run away from them. That's how you give them power! You're continuously confirming they are indeed something dangerous.

We only run away from things that are dangerous.

That's why the "let's do this" technique is so powerful. And trust me, it's not just used by kids. Each and every day, some people say "I do" even though the divorce rate is through the roof, people move to a different state or country because they want a new challenge, people start businesses or invest all of their savings in a home, or they decide to get a divorce and start with a clean slate, they get a new job and leave a secure paycheck behind. Each and every day millions of people are taking risks that undoubtedly give them at least some fear. But they do it anyway! You might have done some of these, felt the fear, and took it with you without fearing the fear itself. You wanted a certain result, you knew fear was a byproduct, and you didn't care.

The only fears that stick around are the ones you choose to fear. The ones where you didn't use the "let's do this!" technique.

This technique is really simple by the way. You say, "Let's do this. Bring it on!" and you do that what you fear, *with* fear.

Did you ever jump from a high diving board into a pool? If you did, then you know it feels scary. But there's a point, right before you jump, where you say, "Let's do this!" You accept the consequences, and you jump. Ah, what a liberating feeling. That's another example of the "whatever happens, it's OK attitude."

The "let's do this" technique is pure exposure with a twist. It's the intention to meet the fear, feel the fear, and then embrace it. Heck, the goal of the technique is for the fear to be as big as possible, so you can find out what will happen on the other side once and for all!

Rianne was a client of mine who had severe dizzy spells in public places like while she was standing in line at the bank or at the checkout counter in the supermarket. When she first met me she often told me "and that's when I *had* to get out of there and just went for the exit" or "that's when I *had* to pop a Xanax to get better."

I explained to her that she was feeding the fear. In her case, even though she could have picked any of the techniques described throughout this book or my audio course, I asked her to specifically use the "let's do this technique." I asked her to go look for a queue, a long one. I told her to get in line and think, "OK, dizziness, come on! Bring it on. Let's do this! I'm not waiting here to get to the front of the line. I'm waiting here for you, dear dizziness!"

"Wow, I'm not sure I can do this," Rianne told me.

I asked her what's the worst that can happen? The absolute worst?

"Well," she said. "I could faint and people will think I'm weak!"

"OK," I said. "If you now compare all of the limiting anxiety you've felt for years, all of the depressing moments you've had because of this fear, what's worse: people seeing you faint once and worst case having a good laugh about it, or you continuing to feel that fear for decades to come?"

"Oh, that fear without a doubt," she replied. That was all she needed in order to give it a try.

She sent me an e-mail a couple of days later with lots of smiley faces and a very upbeat tone of voice. She had found a long queue and as expected, the dizziness came quickly.

Her negative voice tried to take over and asked her to leave as quickly as she could. "NO," she said this time. "If I faint here in front of all of these people, so be it. I want to see what happens. Bring it on, let's do this!"

To her big surprise, the dizziness increased.

"This isn't working," her negative voice jumped in quickly, ready to help as always. "Get out of here!"

"NO," she repeated. "I don't care whether it's working or not, I want you to get bigger, bring it on! Show me what you've got."

This time, the dizziness didn't increase. It had already reached its peak, "Come on," she added. "Is that all you got? Bring it on! Let's do this!"

She started to feel stronger and stronger. About ten minutes into this experience, the dizziness started to subside.

Nothing bad had happened. She didn't run; she didn't pop a pill. She did nothing besides using the "let's do this" technique. And the dizziness and other symptoms went away *on their own*.

The next day she tried again, still savoring the victory she had had the day before. Sure enough, the dizziness came, but this time it only lasted for a minute or two. Two days later, there was no dizziness at all. She couldn't believe it. All of these years she had been trying to avoid her anxiety when all she had to do was embrace it, accept it, and say, "Whatever, I give up. Show me what you got."

Well... it had nothing.

The moment you courageously say, "Bring it on. Let's do this!" is the moment you've just won the first of a couple of battles. **Your intentions have changed!**

Like the kid, you've decided you will no longer run, dodge, or do anything other than embrace it. You have decided to no longer fear the fear. And that's the natural way to overcome anxiety. This is how we've been programmed all along.

When our amygdala or another part of our brain thinks something is a danger, we can say, "You're right!" and run for the hills or search for the exit. This keeps the anxiety and panic attack in place. We've just proven it *was* dangerous by running. The anxiety will now rise each and every time we get into a similar situation. But it's also the moment to say, "No, no, that's not something to be afraid of! That's not a real and imminent threat like being chased by a swarm of African killer bees!"

If anxiety is currently limiting parts of your life, create the intention to live your life, to face those fears, to embrace them—not to control, manage, or avoid—but to truly embrace them and immerse yourself. If and when you do, they will go away (but again, that's not the goal. It can't be or you would be feeding the anxiety).

I know what I've just described is scary, by definition, so please do feel free to use any or all of the other techniques in combination with the "let's do this" technique I defined in this chapter.

Some fears however don't allow you to expose yourself to them. People who fear diseases or serious health problems for instance don't need to try and catch that dangerous flu or whatever they fear.

Here too, however, it's the mindset that counts. The "whatever happens, it's OK" is still at play. I feared having a heart attack when I was an agoraphobic, and I had a slight preference to not expose myself to one. I could nevertheless still use the "whatever happens, it's OK" attitude and decided to say, "I'll let my heart do whatever it wants to do. If this is my moment to go, so be it. Bring it on!" And of course, nothing happened. The grim reaper still didn't come for me.

If you *choose* to no longer fear the worst possible outcome, fear will no longer have any grip on you.

Use Your Imagination

Studies show that our minds don't know the difference between what's real and what we vividly imagine. That's why nightmares can feel so real and even give physical symptoms like waking up in a sweaty full state of panic.

Our imagination is strong. A study done at the University of Ohio in 2014 showed we can actually get muscle growth by vividly imagining we're working out our muscles.[8] Can you picture it? Building muscle by vividly imagining you're working out. Our bodies operate in ridiculously interesting ways.

What we imagine has a profound effect on our entire body and the emotions we feel.

Elite athletes have used this method for a very long time. Even to this day, racecar drivers will simulate the circuit in their head. They close their eyes and imagine driving around the track, steering, braking, shifting, and more. This prepares their body and their mind.

When they're then on the real track, it will feel as if they've just done a couple of practice runs already. Because they did! I'll show you how you can use your imagination in relation to anxiety, phobias, and panic attacks in this chapter.

The first trick is to use meditation. Some people are apprehensive when they hear this word because they link it to spirituality or certain religions. It's totally unrelated, and I'll prove it. Not that there's anything wrong with spirituality by the way.

You can download the relaxation session that comes with the audio course that my clients follow, for free, right here: geertbook.com. I will send you the links to the most recent version. Please download it and put it on an MP3 player, your smartphone, or your tablet.

---

[8] http://jn.physiology.org/content/112/12/3219 Journal of Neurophysiology Published 15 December 2014 Vol. 112 no. 12, 3219-3226 DOI: 10.1152/jn.00386.2014

You can use this session to simply relax, however, this relaxation session serves another major goal. An interesting study found that meditation and other forms of relaxation have the power to shrink the amygdala, thus allowing you to become much more calm, cool, collected and more importantly, confident.[9]

As you may remember, your amygdala is the anxiety-radar you have built into your head. If the amygdala is large and active, a lot of dangers will be seen.

Whilst most studies looked at brain activity *during* meditation, one study from the University of Boston looked at brain scans before and twelve weeks *after* meditation.[10] They found that test persons had a significant decrease in their stress response twelve weeks after having meditated. Not only that, their amygdala, the center of fear, had actually shrunk. How amazing! Meditation is making physical changes in our body that help us face life much better.

As you are relaxing and meditating a bit, there is another way you can use your imagination. In your imagination, you're the director of what happens. So you can imagine doing what scares you and not experiencing any problems. The worst outcome doesn't happen, on the contrary, the best possible outcome appears.

For example, someone afraid of public speaking sees herself giving a speech in front of a large audience. As the speech went smoothly, she gets a standing ovation and loud applause

---

[9] Britta Hölzel et al., "Stress Reduction Correlates with Structural Changes in the Amygdala," Social Cognitive and Affective Neuroscience 5, No. 1 (2010): 11-17.

[10] Effects of mindful-attention and compassion meditation training on amygdala response to emotional stimuli in an ordinary, non-meditative state, Front. Hum. Neurosci., 01 November 2012 | https://doi.org/10.3389/fnhum.2012.00292

that goes on and on. Someone with a fear of flying gets on a plane and sees himself having fun with the crew or sees herself smiling and sitting totally relaxed in her seat.

As you'll use this technique, you can choose to experience everything from your own perspective (first person) or from a camera standpoint, as if you're looking at yourself doing it from a third perspective. Pick whatever works best for you.

With this technique, you'll train your mind to experience what scares you over and over again, without anything going wrong. If and when you then face the situation you fear in real life, your mind/body will also think, "I've been here, I've got this! Nothing bad happened the last X times I was here."

If you've never used your imagination like this, I bet you're skeptical. That's OK, everyone is. You, however, already have a lot of experience with this technique. Every time you thought "what if?" and imagined everything going wrong, you were using your imagination to make it worse. We're using the same system here but in the opposite way. You've seen the negative powers of using your imagination. Now let's use the positive side.

Please try this for at least four weeks. It takes a while before you'll get the desired result because you are reprogramming the way your mind responds to that specific situation. You'll start to see it's very powerful.

On a side note, before I had my Lasik eye surgery a decade ago, I went in for a first appointment a couple of months prior to the surgery, to see if I was eligible. There was a large TV in the waiting room with live footage from the operation currently taking place by the surgeon. Yes, you could see the eye get cut open and then lasered, live.

At first, I didn't get it. I thought, "Does the surgeon not want to have any clients left? Does he really want to scare everyone away by showing real live pictures of knives and lasers cutting into eyes? Most horror movies even stay away from the good old eye cutting... Why not show some funny cat videos instead?"

Only now as I'm writing this book does it dawn on me why he did that. He was exposing everyone to the surgery. Everyone had one or two appointments prior to the operation, and then the day of the operation the TV would be there too.

By the time I was on that table ready to get my eyes done, I had seen about ten surgeries. My mind was ready. I wasn't afraid. Cutting my hair and cutting my eyes felt like the exact same thing to me. Well, almost.

Yes, our minds indeed work in ridiculous ways.

How to Feel Safe Wherever You Are

Feeling at ease wherever you are can drastically reduce your overall stress level and especially the load you put on your central nervous system. It also creates a life that's more enjoyable. Just imagine when "wherever you are" becomes your safe place.

This is something I personally had to practice a lot. When I was an agoraphobic, I only felt safe in my own house, and even there, panic attacks started to plague me. The farther I was from my safe spot, the more my anxiety rose. It was necessary for me to learn to feel at home wherever I was and not even need restrooms or other places I could run to.

While I was working on overcoming my agoraphobia, anxiety, and panic attacks, I had to think of something my aunt once told me when I was about six years old.

She heard me singing while I was walking through her house and said, "Geert, I like how you feel at home wherever you are." She was right. Aside from staying over at her house, I often joined my aunt and uncle on vacation and wherever I was, was my home. I always felt safe and didn't worry, regardless of the situation I was in.

"That kid is still inside you," I thought.

But there was more work to do. I wanted to feel at home *even* when my mind would think of all of the bad possible outcomes related to where I was.

That's the difference. At the age of six I hadn't seen how bad the world could be, how tough it is out there. I had no scars yet and very little negative experiences. I hadn't even touched a warm iron for the first time or tried to cuddle a furry bumblebee. So it's pretty logical my mind wasn't warning me too often. If it only knew...

Still, even at the age of six, the world was a dangerous place, yet I was living in it with full confidence and lots of fun. It is always our perception that makes the difference.

I decided to install a new belief: "I always have me, with me. And that's all I need. Me. My mind. I myself am the safe person. I don't need anyone else, nor do I need another place I can run to."

I engrained this new belief both by using it as an affirmation and by repeating it whenever my negative voice tried to stir up agoraphobic thoughts.

I started to feel at home again, wherever I was. And if anything bad would happen, I would deal with it then and there. I wouldn't flee or search for a safe spot. Then and there would be fine, wherever that was.

Was I right? Yes. Because in the end, my home wasn't any safer or more unsafe than anywhere else. Fainting, losing consciousness, vomiting, dying and all the things I feared would be as bad for my health regardless of where I was. The only difference was that, at home, other people wouldn't see it. There would be no social stigma.

Was the opinion of other people *that* valuable that I was willing to live most of my life in my own home, foregoing plenty of great experiences we should all have as human beings? After years of being an agoraphobic, I finally decided it wasn't. I had had enough of my overgeneralizing.

I had been living with the illusion that everyone *only* liked me if I didn't faint or make a fool out of myself.

It turns out there will always be three groups of people: those who dislike you, those who are indifferent or undecided, and those who like you.

It's impossible to become a version of you that would eradicate the group that dislikes you. That group will always be there. This realization helped me a lot. I could stop trying to be so perfect. If nobody dislikes you, you must be living under a rock. As soon as you come into contact with other people, some will love you, some will like you, some won't care, some will dislike you, and some will hate you for no reason at all. That's how it has always been. Whenever you come in contact with other people, you'll be classifying *them* into these groups as well (liking, loving, indifferent, disliking).

Plus, what other people think of you has nothing to do with you and everything to do with *them*.

Open a great bottle of red wine and let two people taste it. One can like it; the other can tell you she prefers white wine. This says nothing about the wine, and everything about the opinions, likes, and dislikes these two people have.

On top of that, if we ever *do* say something foolish or act foolishly and other people freak out about it, that's really their responsibility and not ours. We cannot control their freaking out or lack thereof.

How to Deal with a Fear of Failure

As with most fears, fear of failure is just another way that your mind can play tricks on you.

In general, the thought process will go like this: "I'm not going to make it/pass, and then bad things will happen. People will think I'm weak or a loser, I don't want to ruin the great image people have of me or I won't get this or that and my life will be pretty abysmal from there on out." This is a clear example of catastrophizing, a mind game.

The true cause of fear of failure and the inability to proceed is the weight you put on the outcome.

Let's look at an example. An area most men have, for instance, felt a fear of failure in is walking up to a woman, introducing themselves and asking for her phone number.

How come?

The two causes are the weight they put on the outcome and what they decide a failure is.

Here's what a typical guy could then think: "If I introduce myself to her and she dismisses me, if I ask for her phone number and she says no, if she doesn't like me... I'll be a loser. I'll then be sure that I will never find a great girlfriend and have confirmation that I'm a loser. Right now, I'm at least a legend in my own mind. Having it confirmed that I'm not the greatest man alive would hurt so much that I prefer to not even find out what she'll say. I need to avoid the pain that would come with the possible rejection. So forget about it, I'm staying here, standing alone in the corner, looking at my phone and pretending to be busy and important. That's what legends do!"

If that's your belief, you wouldn't walk over and introduce yourself to a potential romantic partner. The risk and pain are too high indeed. Getting rejected would set in motion the end of everything, and who in their right mind wants that to happen?

And I'm using a relationship example here, but you can of course apply this to all things where you're afraid to take the next step, out of risk of failure and impending doom.

As always, this problem is created in our own heads. What we say to ourselves is always crucial. If your life will be over whenever something you partake in doesn't go as planned, how on earth would you ever be able to do it without fear? If it's *that* important, you should fear it, lie awake, and worry about it constantly!

Or should you?

Of course not! Most often failing wouldn't be a disaster at all. If our nervous guy with sweaty armpits would walk up to 200 women and introduce himself, 199 could tell him to take a hike, buy some deodorant, and reject him, but one could turn out to be the best girlfriend he could ever have dreamed of. Would those rejections then be a bad thing? Of course not. Every rejection would lead him closer to "the one."

That's how successful actresses and actors dealt with their first castings. That's how successful businessmen and women make deals. It's just life. If you want to succeed, you need to fail often. The definition of failure, however, is crucial.

Thomas Edison invented the light bulb only after he failed hundreds, even thousands of times. To him, however, this wasn't failure. It was a necessity since every faulty bulb brought him a step closer to the one that would do the trick. He said, "I have not failed, I just found 10,000 ways that don't work."

Do you fear failure?

If so, then it might be time to update your belief system. For me personally, failure means not trying. That's when I fail, only then. As long as I try, the result doesn't matter. When something doesn't work out, I learn a valuable lesson, pivot a bit, and change my approach. I go for it again and again...

The "whatever happens, it's OK" attitude is strong here too. If you don't fear the outcome, whatever the outcome would be, there will be no fear to fail.

A guy who decides to not walk up to women to avoid the pain of rejection wins in the short term: no pain. He, however, loses in the long term considering he will never get a decent romantic life. This pain will ultimately be greater than getting rejected every now and then.

A woman who avoids job interviews or starting her own business because she's too afraid she will fail, successfully avoids the pain in the short term. But the long-term pain of not exploring her full potential will hurt a whole lot more in the end.

There are two ways we can use this principle. First, we need to combine it with the fact that our bodies will do what they can to avoid pain. Then we use this as a strategy to motivate ourselves.

Here's how it works, with a personal example. Many years ago I entered the postal office and as I was waiting in line, I saw a woman I liked. She looked at me and smiled. I thought, "I must talk to her" and of course, my negative radio turned on and warned me of all of the reasons why I shouldn't do it (the fact that this was a public setting and that other people would see my downfall played a major role).

If I would have let this system run its course, I would have done nothing. Then, as I would be driving home, negative thoughts like "I'm such a loser. I should have walked over and talked to her. *Next* time I'll do it" would have popped up.

Enter part two of the technique. As I was waiting in line, I started to deliberately imagine everything that would go wrong by *not* talking to her.

- I would think I'm a loser afterward
- I would miss out on getting to know her better
- I would miss out on taking long walks in nature with her
- I would miss out on waking up to her face on the pillow next to me

This, of course, represents pain as well. And because my mind wants to avoid pain, it found the motivation to walk over and talk to her, even though my heart was beating out of my chest. This very woman became my girlfriend, and I've now been happily living with her for many years.

Nevertheless, it almost never happened because of my fear of failure.

What areas of your life could and should you apply this technique in?

When your mind comes up with everything that can go wrong, overrule that by imagining what you will miss out upon by not doing it.

How to No Longer Care What People Think of You

I don't know what fears you suffer from, but chances are they are in some way linked to other people. This is definitely the case should you suffer from a social phobia, agoraphobia, the nice guy/girl syndrome, or any other fear based upon, "Oh no! What will *they* think of me when... "

If you have no trouble at all with this, you can skip this chapter.

Since you're still reading, you probably face these three difficulties:

1. You fear what strangers think of you.
2. You fear what people you know somewhat think of you.
3. You fear what people you know really well think of you.

Options one and two should be dismissed right away. If you care about the opinions of people in groups one and two, you'll overburden your processor. There are too many people to worry about. Repeat that to yourself whenever these fears surface.

Also understand that everyone will have haters. There is no way to avoid that. Even if you lay low and try to not have a conflict with anyone, conflicts will find you.

If I ask you to think about the one person you know at work or at school—or wherever you're part of a larger group of people—the one person who's the most respected and the most charismatic, who would that be?

Do you have someone in mind? Someone everyone (including you) respects and admires.

Now, the question is: is that person a people pleaser? Is that person flawless and perfect?

No.

People caring a lot about what others think of them do not get the respect and love they so desperately crave. It's a rule of life. One I didn't like at first, to be honest, since I am a former people pleaser. But we can't fight the rules of life.

Whenever I bring out a new YouTube video or any other form of content, for about every twenty good comments or feedback I get, I get a rude or a negative one. I could try to adapt and avoid that one rude comment. But it's not worth it; it's not even possible. That rude comment says more about the person who posted it than it says about my performance in the video.

Rude comments come from people filled with hate and negativity. They are clearly not in a happy place for one reason or another. That's why they cannot be avoided. Some people you come into contact with will feel miserable for some reason or even no reason at all. It will be easy to upset them, make them lash out, and make them treat you badly. All of this has nothing to do with you, what you said, or what you did. It's on them.

Some people try to avoid conflicts or getting hurt. These two are unavoidable. Whether you have a tendency to assertively stand up for yourself or you suffer from the disease to please, conflicts will arise and you will get hurt. It's a law of life.

Remarkably, people pleasers who try to avoid getting hurt end up getting hurt a lot more often, because other people start taking them for granted and treat them like a doormat.

If you want to live your life, have experiences that matter, and have fun every now and then, you'll always cross the path of people who won't agree with you or who will be rude in some way. Apply the "whatever happens, it's OK" attitude. It's a part of life; it cannot be avoided.

If that's the way *they* want to go through life, I feel sorry for them. I pity them. These negative-minded people are clearly unhappy. Their lives must be *so* bad that they need to vent that negativity and will let it impact others. Silly, isn't it?

But therein lies the secret. There's nothing you could possibly do to transform these people into positive versions that will like and love you. It's a waste of time. It's not our job to educate or change other people.

I could write a whole other book on people-pleasing and the many reasons why you should never try it. Let me pick the one reason that matters here: it will make you stressed out and anxious.

Every negative emotion you have makes you more prone to anxiety. Trying to please other people by adapting to their wishes and whims and trying to be a chameleon that changes his/her behavior to blend in and be liked (or not seen at all), demands a tremendous amount of energy. And for what? For something that cannot be avoided!

You've heard the timeless adage, "Just be yourself."

Who is that anyway?

I apply it in the sense that I no longer adapt in an effort to be liked. When I still was an agoraphobic, I thought everyone was continuously judging me. From the people I would cross on the street and didn't even know to the close friends and colleagues I looked up to.

When I walked into a room of people, I could feel and hear the hundreds of possible opinions of everyone glancing over. As I talked to someone, I tried to get inside of their minds so I could figure out if I was pleasing them and if they liked what I said. I continuously sought their approval.

And you know what? None of that mattered. Those who liked me, liked me; those who didn't, didn't. I, on the other hand, was wasting energy and fun I could have had. I was quickly depleting my batteries whenever I did something that involved the presence of other people. This had turned me into a Highly Sensitive Person (HSP). There were too many triggers and stimuli I continuously had to take into account. Micro expressions on other people's faces, what they were saying, how they were saying it, the way they looked at me...

While I was overcoming my phobias and anxieties, I was sitting in a movie theater—the place where I feared getting nauseated and vomiting in front of other people. Surely, because my mind had been conditioned, my thoughts went there again, "Yep, there you have it. You're nauseous. What if you now start to throw up? Isn't it best you leave now, right away?" That's what I would have done in the past. Heck, I probably wouldn't even have been there.

"STOP!" I thought. Instead, I chose to say to myself, "Whatever happens, it's OK. If I vomit, projectile style, and I cover all of the people in front of me including the movie screen, so be it. BRING IT ON! I don't care anymore. I'm sick and tired of this type of anxiety. I want to live, and I don't want to adapt any longer. So I'm going to make the <u>choice</u> to not care! Bring it on, whatever it will be. And if all of these people hate me, so be it! These guys are just movie extras filling up the room. They're nothing but other elements of nature."

"When I walk in the woods, do I care about what the trees think of me? NO! Well, people are—just like trees—elements of nature. The sun will still come up tomorrow; the birds will still fly around and chirp. Traffic jams will still appear everywhere. Life goes on. So who cares? Why should I spend energy on this? **Because you know what's worse? If I continue to do what I always do, I'm going to talk down to myself, be disappointed, think I'm a loser and a failure. I would have a bad opinion of myself. And that's the only opinion that ever matters. My own opinion. And I like me. I love me. These other people are just extras filling up the room. So be it."**

What a rant! But a good one.

As I was using this positive self-dialogue, convincing myself why I shouldn't care about what others thought of me, I felt a form of power grow in me that took over. The nausea didn't subside right away, but the anxiety did. I was free.

I truly didn't care about others anymore. I had finally managed to turn the switch. I then started to apply this exact way of thinking wherever my search for approval tried to take over.

How can you apply this in your life? Please do a little exercise where you write down your limiting beliefs related to being liked by other people. When that's done, answer the way I just did in that movie theater. Write down the script you will be using the next time you're limiting yourself by seeking the approval of others too much. Write it down beforehand or afterward (for the next time), but please, write it down.

A Special Word on Panic Attacks

Using your mind to deal with anxiety is one thing, employing your mind to deal with panic attacks will often be a bit trickier since your mind and entire body are in "Death is imminent! Help!" mode.

It's hard to reason with yourself when your mind and body are in that zone. So although I want you to use all of the other techniques and mindsets already explained before (they will help, even with severe panic attacks!), here are some specific thoughts you can unleash on panic attacks and the negative self-talk that comes with them.

- "I'm going to die!"
- "Is this a heart attack?"
- "I'm about to faint."
- "I need to get out of here NOW!"
- "Must be a disease, a bad one!"
- "I'm going to lose my mind, I may have already lost it!"

If the symptoms you are feeling are severe, any of these sentences will probably be one of your first thoughts. Let's focus on the most dominant symptom most people have: the heart rate goes up. You may have a different symptom. What follows still applies to you too. When you panic, you always panic about something. It will often be a symptom, a sensation, you may panic about the situation you're in, the fact that you can't get out when you please or any one of the other millions of possibilities. We'll deal with more symptoms in the addendum at the back of the book.

For this example, however, we'll presuppose your heart rate goes up and this triggers the first thought of, "What's going on here? I hope that... " This can eventually launch the vicious cycle.

First of all, the fact that you're feeling a symptom may not mean anything. There are so many reasons why your heart rate might go up without there being anything wrong with your heart. Some examples include: you have some internal anger, you ate chocolate (the substance theobromine in the cacao increases the heart rate), you ate something that your body is slightly allergic to, you drank alcohol, you're stressed, you're about to catch the flu or a cold, you're nervous about an upcoming event, and so on.

You may of course also feel the symptoms because of the anxiety itself.

The symptoms will all have a logical cause. It's your body reacting to something or your body that's taking care of a task it has to complete. If that, however, starts to worry you, then you launch the vicious panic attack cycle as I've explained in part one of the book.

Let's say you then start to worry about the symptoms themselves, in combination with the fact that they are appearing in the most inappropriate moment (in a restaurant, during a meeting, in flight, at home alone, while far away from home, while surrounded by other people).

I'm not a doctor, and having symptoms can mean something *is* wrong. Nonetheless, if you've had your health checked by a medical doctor like I've asked you to, then know that you are not dying when you feel any or all of these symptoms. The panic attack that's giving you these unwanted sensations is the very system that wants to keep you alive.

Trust in the verdict your doctor gave you. When he or she said you are healthy and medically fine, you are. Doctors have been trained for many years; they don't overlook serious health problems. It's simply because the fight-or-flight system has been activated that you are feeling some strange symptoms.

Your negative voice might now say, "Doctors *do* miss things. They're human beings! I've heard stories and seen stuff on TV and the Internet... " If you had that thought, that's again proof of your incredibly powerful radar that looks out for you. It's trying to find BS in what I'm saying in order to protect you. It's doing its job!

Yes. Of course it has happened that a doctor told a patient, "You're fine and superbly healthy," and that patient then walks out and dies upon getting in his or her car. True. A piano may have landed on his head, an angry mob of vicious scorpions may have stung him, he may have had a heart attack... People are dying every second for a variety of reasons. People are winning the lottery every second. People are making the best love they ever made every second. People are doing a gazillion things every single second of the day.

But that's not the point. If you have symptoms that worry you, it is your responsibility to have your health checked by a professional. It is *not* your responsibility to freak out, have anxiety, and continuously worry about it.

Ever since I've overcome my panic attacks, I do get struck by odd symptoms every now and then, and it can happen at an inappropriate moment too. Not often, but it does happen. When it does I follow the following script:

1. I say, "whatever happens, it's OK. I choose to not feel anxiety. Having the symptom is bad enough. I don't need to add oil to the fire. Been there done that."

2. If the symptom is really bad or weird or persists, I go see my doctor.

3. I trust my doctor's verdict, or, if the feeling stays, I may look for a solution elsewhere. But I do not freak out about it! I no longer feel anxiety for it.

Again, if I were to die right now while typing this sentence, I would have peace with that. Totally ridiculous to some, not to me. I've had a fear of death for fourteen years, and trust me, *that* was ridiculous. I forgot to live. And now, almost two decades later, I'm still alive and kicking.

All of that worrying was for nothing, time I could have spent learning how to knit my own sweaters or how to singlehandedly stop global warming. Plus, even *if* bad stuff is about to happen, worrying won't save us.

So if you get a strange sensation, choose not to fear it. It's a tough choice since the anxiety won't fall away immediately upon making the choice, but at least you won't pour oil on the fire. And little by little the symptoms won't launch anxiety any longer.

Please, I know this is very easy to say and overwhelmingly hard to do. I've had to go through it, and I've seen many of my clients wrestle with it too. But standing on the other side and looking back, I can tell you it's worth the struggle.

You can take it one step at a time. What you can do is figure out what is causing your symptoms, if you can. Was it something you ate? Are there major changes in your life? Have you caught a cold or another virus? How did you sleep the night before? Do you have too much on your plate? The answers to these questions can help you pinpoint why it's happening.

Then, add any of the techniques you've learned in part two (making fun of it, making it more ridiculous, using a softer version of the "whatever happens, it's OK" like the "if this turns out to be something bad, I'll worry about it when I'm sure, not before.")

Two separate programs are running here:

1. The symptom you are feeling probably doesn't mean anything. Your doctor can help you find out. However, even though it could have a medical cause, that still doesn't mean you should...

2. ...add anxiety on top of it. This has nothing to do with the actual symptom. <u>Anxiety is a choice</u>. And this is where you have the mental power to make a different one.

You decide what you give weight to and what thoughts you follow. The negative voice just gives you options that you are free to decline, as you've learned earlier.

Here are some of the options your negative voice will have on the menu:

"Am I going to lose consciousness or will I faint?"

Needless to say, the solution to this remains, "Whatever happens, even if I faint, so be it. It's OK. I'll deal with it when and *if* it happens."

Now before you get there and master this "whatever" way of thinking, take baby steps and explain to your negative voice that the panic attack system is exactly there so you would *not* faint.

It's the fight-or-flight system, not the faint system. It's rushing blood to your muscles (and thus takes it away from your brain, which explains the light-headedness) so you can punch that danger to the ground or outrun a leopard (or at least try to) if need be. Fainting would get you killed, so it's not on the menu during an actual panic attack.

"I need to get the *&%! out of here."

Look around. Are you surrounded by a real threat? If yes, please do get out of there quickly. If not—and this is obviously the most probable outcome—stay. Let it come. Decide to no longer let your life be dictated by the panic attacks. From now on, you no longer run from them. The anxiety and panic attacks don't get to decide when you leave, what experiences you miss, how low or high the quality of your life is. *You* do!

If the panic attack comes, you take it with you. You'll smother it with so much acceptance and love, it will eventually grow tired of accompanying you!

Besides the "whatever happens it's OK," it's also beneficial to say, "Bring it on. I'm going to stay, and I want to see what happens. Let's find out if it really *is* as bad as my negative voice wants me to believe." This is powerful, and I've discussed it in detail before.

What you're feeling during a panic attack is already the pinnacle of what anxiety has in store. It cannot get worse; you're already there.

Furthermore, a full-blown panic attack can only last a couple of minutes. The adrenaline you're feeling will be taken back up by organs like your liver; it will pass! Even *if* you stay.

Do you know what the benefit of leaving is? Why does your anxiety often calm down when you do leave?

Once you reach your safe place, you'll probably think it's over. You're saved. As a result, your anxiety will drop. Can you see why?

It's because you told yourself so! You calmed yourself down by telling yourself you're safe. The physical danger, in that safe place, is as small as it was in the place you were previously in. So why not stay there and calm your mind and body down there, on the spot?

It works just as well. And the added benefit is that you won't have to keep avoiding that location in the future. At first, it will take you five to twenty minutes to calm down, which is a bit more than if you sought out the exit and left. But the long-term consequences are so much better since you communicate to your mind and body that you no longer fear the fear.

And that's always the best choice to make.

The Body

The body is an often overlooked part of most panic attack and anxiety treatments. Whenever I visited my doctor while I still suffered from panic attacks, agoraphobia, social phobia, and generalized anxiety disorder, my doctor never talked about my body or asked anything about how I was treating it. I've explained before that my dog's vet always asked what I had been feeding him. I wondered why my doctor never asked me about this.

Thinking of my dog, Amadeus, and the effect food apparently had on his symptoms and ailments, I wondered if many of the strange sensations and symptoms I had (the ones where the doctor always told me, "You're fine, Geert. You're in great health. I can't find anything. Bye bye!") were actually caused by what I was eating and drinking.

I started a food log and diary, and every time I felt a strange symptom like a headache, dizziness, nausea, tingling sensations, dry mouth, or anything else, I noted:

- What I had been eating/drinking up to 24 hours prior to the symptom
- What I had smelled up to 24 hours prior to the symptom (perfumes, chemical odors, new car smell, paint, new furniture, old building smell, musky smells)
- What I had applied on my skin or otherwise been in physical contact with (shampoo, shaving cream, toothpaste)
- Where I had been
- What I had been thinking about (the negative thoughts I had had)

It took me a couple of weeks until I began to see the first possible correlations. I had a serious headache every time I drank a diet drink with an artificial sweetener. I felt nauseated a couple of hours after I had smelled new car smell, regular laundry detergent, certain perfumes, and other toxic smells. MSG, yeast extract, and other taste enhancers made me nauseous and dizzy. My fluoride-containing toothpaste made me nauseous and light-headed, and shampoos and soaps with sodium lauryl sulfate and other toxins gave me severe vertigo as soon as thirty minutes after using them.

My body was reacting to a lot of substances. And when I read *Never Be Sick Again* by Raymond Francis, what I had been suspecting was confirmed. If you have a chemical overload in your body, you can feel very sick, even *be* very sick. And in some cases, your doctor will not find anything. Your body is fine but became hyper sensitive to certain chemicals and unnatural substances. More and more people have chemical sensitivities these days because our cells are confronted with more toxic substances than ever before in the history of mankind.

What you react to might be different, but in the more than ten years I've been helping people who suffered from panic attacks and anxiety, I've seen that a lot of people were in fact reacting to certain ingredients, especially sensitive people plagued by unwanted anxiety and weird bodily sensations their doctors cannot explain. Starting the abovementioned diary can help, because your body is always communicating what it likes and dislikes.

Aside from that, we can also use the body to significantly alleviate anxiety.

Abdominal Breathing

Almost every therapist will teach you abdominal breathing. Although it is somewhat helpful, it is not sufficient to overcome anxiety. That's fine. I suggest you still use it. Abdominal breathing helps because it would be impossible to breathe calmly through the abdomen as you are running for your life while being chased by a real predator.

By choosing to breathe slowly through the abdomen, you're communicating to your entire body and especially the amygdala that the anxiety response was wrong and that there is no danger. As we've seen there are many ways to communicate to the amygdala that it was wrong. Here we're using the body to do so.

You can practice abdominal breathing by lying down on your back, by putting one hand on your chest and the other hand on your tummy. As you breathe in and out, only the hand on your tummy should move. You can find lots of clips on YouTube showing you how to practice abdominal breathing, and we also do it in the relaxation session you can download from my website, on: geertbook.com

You breathe in slowly through the nose for about 3-5 seconds. Then you hold your breath for another 3-5 seconds. Then you breathe out through the mouth for about 4-8 seconds.

If you practice this enough while you're in a calm state of mind, this breathing pattern will slowly start to become your new way of automatic breathing throughout the day. When you're anxious, however, and especially if you're experiencing a panic attack, you will be breathing from your chest. This will be increasing the anxiety and possibly even pushing you into hyperventilation mode (where you get too much oxygen in your blood). At that point, consciously decide to practice your abdominal breathing.

At first, this will freak your body out. As you start to breathe slower, your heart rate will go up *even more*. Don't stop then! Your body is simply screaming, "No, no! There's no time for abdominal breathing now, what are you thinking? DANGER! I need blood in the muscles!"

Hang in there. You need to have the final word. If you continue to practice the abdominal breathing at that time, even though your body gives you a whole range of nervous sensations, your body will soon start to listen and calm down.

That said, you'll need to apply other techniques as well. Abdominal breathing alone is not sufficient. That's why this is not the only chapter in this book.

Exercise

I bet I'm not the first one to tell you that you need to exercise to have a healthy body and mind. Yes, *they*—the ones who have been advocating this forever—were right and there really is no way around it. I used to be lazy, so believe me, I've looked. If you don't fatigue the body by moving around and working out, the excess energy will often surface under the form of anxiety or general nervousness. But there are many more processes in the body, such as your insulin resistance and other hormones, that will perform much better too.

In my more than a decade of helping people, exercise proved to be a very potent anti-anxiety tool for *everyone* who gave it a try.

Exercise is a two-edged sword, however. Some people go too far and make themselves prone to anxiety and panic attacks by stressing out their body. I've had many athletes as clients, who pushed their bodies too far for too long. The physical stress was too great. Excessive stress is too much, be that the physical or the mental version of it.

So what would be a good rule of thumb? It's important you always feel better the day after you've done any form of exercise, not more tired and worn out. If you do feel depleted or sore the day after, decrease the intensity of the exercise.

If you're not working out at all at the moment, choose something simple like using a stationary bike (I use it for fifteen minutes, three times per week). It's OK to put it in front of the TV. The best work out for you is the one where you don't have any excuses not to do it.

I also go for a walk in nature two to three times per week; I walk briskly for about thirty to forty minutes. I choose areas like a field with far views or a forest with lots of birds and plants. As I'm walking, I look at those birds, see the wind going through the trees, and observe the clouds. This is a form of meditation too. It relaxes my entire nervous system since I cannot think about the day's stresses and worries *and* focus on the birds. We've already seen that this can make the amygdala smaller as well.

It's very probable you've already had thoughts like, "I don't have time for that." I get it. Nobody does.

But it is important for many reasons. Harvard Business Review wrote an article in 2015 describing a study performed at the University of Melbourne, Australia, that discovered people who spent time looking at nature, for as little as five minutes, increased their mental performance and productivity.[11]

Another Harvard Business Review article in 2017 cites studies that prove that taking time for silence restores the nervous system. [12] Aha... and that's exactly what anxious people need!

I soon noticed that I was much more effective and got a lot more work done on the days I *did* go for that walk, even though I didn't have time for it. I could work faster and with more concentration compared to the days where I even ate lunch in front of the computer to get more work done. It's an illusion to think that continuous work helps you get more work done. Your attention starts to drift away quickly after about forty-five minutes, and the quality of your work goes down unless you take some time to recharge.

I've made a lot of changes, all based on what my body was telling me. I stopped eating things my body doesn't know how to use; I started to work out just the right amount for my body, and I made sure I had a good night's rest almost every night.

And rest assured, the results my clients have had because of what I describe in this very chapter have been amazing too.

Your body is continuously communicating to you. If you don't feel well, then something is amiss, and you'll need to make some changes.

---

[11] https://hbr.org/2015/09/gazing-at-nature-makes-you-more-productive
[12] https://hbr.org/2017/03/the-busier-you-are-the-more-you-need-quiet-time

Part 3: Putting It into Practice

Now that we've dealt with the causes and you've learned a wide array of techniques, it's time to put them into practice. There are a couple of ways to get started.

Jumping Into the Deep End of the Pool

Do you avoid everything that makes you uneasy or downright anxious? Or do you face your fears?

Do you *expose* yourself to your anxiety and the possible bad outcomes? Or do you run?

Exposure is strong against anxiety because it is your way of saying, "I don't fear the fear. I will feel fear, but I'll do it anyway." That's strong. Running away gives more power to the anxiety, to what you fear.

If you are avoiding supermarkets, driving, social events, meetings, speeches, flying, or just about anything else because you fear getting a panic attack, anxiety, or another symptom, you are telling yourself that those locations are dangerous.

If you avoid that what you fear, you give it power. So in order to overcome the anxiety and get on with your life, there's no other way than to expose yourself to that what you fear so much. If you want to tame a wild horse, you'll have to get on its back and ride it out until the horse accepts you and calms down. If you want to tame the anxiety tiger and turn him into your furry pet, you'll have to get into its cage and risk getting a scratch or two. We've all had to go through this, and this is the way you can break through your anxious conditioning.

It doesn't work the other way around. Everyone hopes and thinks, "I'll wait for my anxiety to pass first, *then* I'll start doing and exposing myself again." That's putting the cart before the horse. It doesn't work like that.

Exposure is one way to reverse the anxious programming. If you keep doing what scares you and nothing happens, your fear will start to decline. There is, however, an exception to this rule that I'll deal with in a bit.

If your mind has linked up the anxiety to a certain place, person, thing, or action, you will always have a raised anxiety level when you expose yourself to it again. This cannot be avoided. You'll have to wean it out slowly and teach your body, step by step, that the anxiety fire alarm is not needed.

Michael is one of my clients. He's a medical doctor, and he had a major fear of driving on any street that had more than two lanes combined. He would make incredible detours to avoid the highway. What he struggled with most was that he felt like a failure. During our first conversation, he told me, "I'm a doctor, Geert. I understand the body. I shouldn't be having this stupid anxiety; it's driving me crazy. I feel like a fraud when I'm helping patients."

Since Michael hadn't been driving on highways for a couple of years, exposure was a big part of his path to get over his fears. I first taught him all of the mental techniques he needed to tackle his anxiety. Once he had memorized those, he started to map out areas where he could go for an on-and-off drive, for real.

He got on the highway and then got back off the next exit. Whenever he wasn't able to manage or decrease his anxiety, which of course happened at first, I asked him to stop the car where it was safe to do so, take out his journal, and write down what his negative voice had been saying.

Then I asked Michael to write down how he could have responded (using the techniques I've already explained earlier on in the book like questioning the thoughts, using humor, etc.).

Next, Michael got back on the same highway and practiced what he'd just written down. He was very hesitant the first couple of times he tried it. But he gained more confidence each and every time until his anxiety started to flow away. A couple of weeks later, Michael was driving everywhere again, even singing some songs on the radio.

This happens to be another way to deal with anxiety. It's impossible to sing a song while being chased by a tiger. So the mere fact that you're singing your favorite song communicates to your body that you are not in any danger. On top of that, it's a great way to use the energy caused by the adrenaline.

Jenna, on the other hand, had a major fear of public spaces. The supermarket was one of her worst spots since there she felt trapped at the checkout counter while she was waiting in line. That's the moment she couldn't run if needed. "People would think I'm a fool or worse, a thief," she said. The only time she'd dare to enter a supermarket was when her boyfriend would accompany her.

What Jenna did was the opposite of exposure. Can you see why?

Bringing her boyfriend with her was empowering her anxiety. She told her subconscious mind, "The supermarket is dangerous. I need my boyfriend to protect me and feel safe."

After learning all of the techniques to defend herself against anxiety (the ones you've gotten in part two), she chose the option of gradual exposure. She went to the supermarket alone a couple of times, without the need to buy anything. She did bring the audio course with her on her phone, so she could listen to my voice when needed. Although she could run away whenever she wanted, I asked her to stay as long as she could, just to see what would happen.

Every time Jenna went, she increased her time spent there. About three weeks later, I got an e-mail from her with the subject line, "I did it!"

Jenna explained she had bought all of her groceries alone, and even though the anxiety had tried to increase, she was able to take control and push it away while she continued to fill up her shopping cart. This was a major victory for her as you can imagine.

I want to elaborate a bit on what happened here and why this helped her out, so you can apply it better as well.

1. As the anxiety came, she didn't run anymore. This was her way of saying, "I choose to no longer have fear of the fear." This is the first positive domino that needs to fall.

2. She let the anxiety flood her. Although the anxiety was there, she didn't start to hurry to get it over with. She waited for the worst to happen. That's the "whatever happens, it's OK" mindset.

3. As time went by, the real tigers didn't appear since they're fonder of the jungle than supermarkets. People didn't yell at her, and none of the bad stuff her negative voice had been warning her about happened.

4. She realized her negative voice was full of it. It wasn't the oracle. She could simply laugh it off the next time.

5. Her intolerance to anxiety decreased significantly. It wasn't something she had to avoid any longer. Anxiety wasn't bad. This last domino was what set her free.

There are many ways you can benefit from exposure. One way is going all in from the get-go. This can be brutal, but it is often very effective since more than one fear can vanish at once.

The second way is a step-by-step process, sometimes even three steps ahead, one backward. That's fine, too. I've seen great results amongst my clients whatever way they chose. All in or slowly working their way up.

If you want to go slow, plan to take it one step at a time. You can include exit strategies for every step of the way. Examples are taking someone with you (who can drive you home, if need be), making sure someone is on standby that you can call whenever needed, and taking tools with you. No hammers and axes but a lifeline. I had a fear of getting nauseous in public places, so at first I would carry a little plastic bag in my pocket, just in case. Those exit strategies are fine. Not needed, but they are fine.

The challenge, however, is to last as long as you possibly can without reaching for them. The very first time Jenna exposed herself to her fears in the supermarket, her boyfriend was waiting for her in the car on the parking lot. That was fine since he didn't join her. He was just the exit strategy. She still faced her fears alone.

If Possible, Don't Plan Ahead

I realize this is not always possible, but it can be helpful to not plan ahead and just do whatever scares you in the heat of the moment. We all have our good and our bad days. Say you are having a good day and you wonder if today is a good day to test that thing that gives you anxiety. That's the moment to jump up and do it.

Really!

As you try to make the decision to go for it, your mind will then continue to play games with you and will still try to stop you. It will give you all of the excuses in the book (logically, it's trying to keep you safe and still thinks that whatever it is you fear includes hungry predators). Don't listen to that voice; it's just another mind game. Go for it!

If you have to plan ahead (e.g., for a fear of public speaking or flying), that's fine too. The anticipatory fear will try to bother *and* stop you, so your mind will keep coming up with the event as it comes closer and will force you to bail out with an excuse. Keep dismissing it, as much as you need to.

"Thanks, warning system. I'll see what happens when the moment comes, not beforehand!"

During your exposure, you'll need to mainly work on three things:

1. Uncertainty
2. Control
3. Anxiety itself

The uncertainty is the reason you have been avoiding that what gives you anxiety. It's exactly because you don't know what will happen that you're anxious. You wonder if your worst nightmare will come true or not. Might the negative voice be right? Will that bad thing really happen? Here too, we've all had to face this uncertainty and in a way say, "You know what? Whatever happens it's OK. Show me what you've got!" This is the best way to accept and even embrace the uncertainty.

That phrase and mindset will also help with **control.** During the exposure, your mind will want you to be in control in an effort to take away the uncertainty (e.g., "Go for the aisle seat so you can get up whenever needed" or "Let's do it when it won't be crowded" or "Let's call in sick."). Let go of the notion of having everything under control, and go with the flow. If you want to take it step-by-step, limit the control you'll have and only build in some contingencies or exit strategies like the people from the examples I previously gave you did.

Letting go of control is crucial to living a life where anxiety doesn't dominate you. It's the solution to a social phobia, a fear of driving or flying, hypochondria, and many more forms of anxiety.

If control is an issue for you, and I bet it is, your mind mistakenly believes that having everything under control will give you the freedom you desire. This is faulty. You cannot have everything under control. There are so many factors we cannot control: nature, the reactions and thoughts of other people, traffic, etc. There are a gazillion things we cannot control, and true freedom comes when you fully embrace *that*. Embracing the fact you cannot control everything can lift a huge weight off your shoulders and set you free. That sounds like it comes from one of those spiritually enlightening books, doesn't it? But it isn't. Trying to have everything under control severely limits your freedom and the quality of your life. Not to mention that it will burn out your nervous system swiftly.

This is a true catch-22. The more you try to have everything under control, the less control you'll have.

Imagine what will happen when your mind comes up with a "what if?" question or any other anxiety inducer, and you automatically dismiss it. Can you imagine how free you would be? How easy would it be to say "yes" to all of the experiences life has to offer without worrying?

The third challenge you'll need to work on is the anxiety itself. Whenever you expose yourself to what you fear, it's logical that you will feel anxiety. Nonetheless, the simple fact that you decide to face your fears is a step of major importance. It communicates to your subconscious mind that you've decided to no longer fear the fear itself. This is very important.

You'll need to be prepared for this third challenge.

I've had clients who started to expose themselves to what they feared, and it went well from the get-go. (This is not the norm.) So they kept doing it and mistakenly thought the problem was gone.

But then at one point, they felt a bout of unexpected anxiety. It was as if lightning struck while the skies were blue. They panicked. They didn't know what to think, so they followed the negative thoughts that popped up, "Oh no, it's back. I'll never get over this..."

You will always need to expect that anxiety will show its head at some point. When you expect it, it won't take you by surprise.

Please remember that it's impossible to live without anxiety. There will always be events that can scare you. We can't turn the alarm system off. And it will still give a false alarm here and there. So it's your intolerance to anxiety that needs to be overcome.

Anxiety is a normal emotion. We can all feel it. "Normal" people, however, don't dislike anxiety. They simply dismiss it when it's not appropriate.

The strategy in this exposure phase is that this time you won't run away or try to get it over with as quickly as you can. You'll stay and face it, so the anxiety can show you how ugly it can get. Then, since you're still there, you'll see your negative thoughts were full of it. They had been bluffing all along.

Let me repeat that. **If you don't run from your anxiety and just wait it out, it will get bad (with or without a panic attack) and then it will pass!**

On its own.

There's no need to run.

To recap: exposure is a powerful and necessary weapon against anxiety, but only when you combine it with the other tools you are learning throughout this book.

When It Tries to Come Back

Since I've been helping people get over their anxiety and panic attacks for so long, I've had thousands of people who overcame their panic attacks and could finally start living their lives again.

Some of them, however, sent me an e-mail often more than five years later stating, "I've had a panic attack. All is lost, right? What do I do now?" That's a very interesting question.

Just imagine what it would feel like: you finally overcome those pesky symptoms and feelings, you start living your life again without that dreaded fear of the fear, and for the first time in ages, you get to *enjoy* doing that what you previously feared.

But then, lightning strikes. You get an anxious moment and possibly a panic attack. Your negative thoughts kick in, and warn you, "There you have it! I'm back at square one. Everything is starting again!"

Honestly, the fact that you *will* have uncomfortable moments in the future is as sure as the fact that ice melts in the desert. It's unavoidable. The question is: how will you respond?

The initial negative thoughts are very normal, you still have your danger radar, you still have your little cartoonish devil, you still have your negative voice. You remain human, after all.

But what you do next will be important. We both know what will happen if you go down the "why, oh why... " path.

It's better to overrule the negative voice with sentences like, "Sure, sure. Whatever happens it's all OK. Panic attack, no panic attack, feeling perfect, not feeling perfect… I go with the flow. I no longer fear the fear. If anxiety wants to come and visit for whatever reason under the sun, it can. I'll just take it with me."

From now on, never fear the fear. Make that decision today.

It's worth it.

Now It's Up to You

When I launched the first version of my audio course in 2005, some people sent me an e-mail asking, "Should I still go through the entire course if I only have one type of anxiety? Can I just go through certain sessions? I'm looking for a shortcut you see."

The answer was and is always yes; every single session of the course is important. I am not a psychic. I have no idea what combination of techniques will work best for someone. All the techniques work together, and it's up to you to specialize and utilize them for your particular needs. You can only get there if you test and apply all of them.

The same applies to this book.

Some of your habits and the ways you deal with your thoughts are causing and maintaining the anxiety that currently holds you back. You'll need to try and test a whole range of techniques to find out what combination works best for you.

Please understand that it took me more than six months to completely overcome my panic attacks. On average, people who follow my audio course need a couple of weeks before they start to feel better and a couple of months before they are "cured." Even then, there is no typical result. It takes time.

So many websites, pills, books, and gurus try to make you believe it's easy and fast to overcome anxiety and panic attacks with their special trick (and that trick, of course, is the *only* solution against panic attacks. Without it, everyone is doomed). These are blatant lies and misleading claims. It's not easy. It's never fast, and there is no *one* solution. Luckily, however, it is very much possible to totally eradicate panic attacks, phobias, and generalized anxiety disorders!

Overcoming anxiety and panic attacks can be compared to climbing a mountain. It won't be easy. There will be setbacks. But when you reach the top, the view will be great. As long as you continue to climb, you *will* reach the top. I want to stress this because I know you're currently still suffering from your negative voice. It's still taunting you. You may have tried a couple of techniques prior to reading this book and felt no change. Don't listen to the negative voice telling you that overcoming your anxiety is impossible. That's not true (and the negative voice can't prove that it *is* anyway)!

This is a challenge we've all faced. I remember Claire, a woman who was following my audio course about seven years ago. After she finished the second session, she sent me an e-mail explaining how great she felt. She had a social phobia and had successfully used some of the techniques during a wedding she attended. She felt so relieved! Her problems were finally over. Although that was indeed a great result, I asked her to stick to the course and to continue working on herself. There was a reason the course consists of multiple sessions, not just two.

Even though she had the entire course at her disposal, she was so happy with that early result that she paused the course. About a month later, she reached out to me again. Claire explained she had had another panic attack. "All of my symptoms are back," she told me. "I got a panic attack yesterday. That spooked me so much. I feel so depressed and disappointed now and can't help but think I'm a lost case. I'll never get over this. What do I do now?"

Before you continue reading. Can you see what happened to her and why? What could she have done better?

She made a couple of logical mistakes we're all prone to make.

1. She paused the course after only two sessions because she had immediate results. That's what she was hoping for: a miracle. When the miracle seemed to come, she stopped putting in an effort. That's like removing some of the weeds in the garden without eliminating the roots. The weeds will come back quickly.

2. She expected her anxiety to never try to resurface once it was gone.

3. She still feared the anxiety and was intolerant to it. There was no acceptance. She still feared the fear. That's the true root!

4. When her anxiety came back, her negative voice went crazy and played many mind games on her. *She believed that voice*

because she hadn't mastered all of the techniques yet.

I like to compare this to learning how to drive. Knowing how to drive a car in a straight line doesn't enable you to handle busy intersections, mountain roads, or traffic jams filled with angry drivers behind the wheel. You need to put in the time and effort to learn how to respond in a variety of situations.

Claire had tried to skip those steps. So I asked Claire to start over and continue the course till the end. Six months later, she e-mailed me back and told me she had completed all of the sessions. She added, "Geert, I know I'm not done yet. I haven't had anxiety for months now, but I'll continue to practice the techniques. And if my anxiety tries to come back, I won't get spooked this time. I'll simply put it back into its cage." Although she did feel anxious once or twice since then (after a difficult divorce, for instance), she managed to keep the unnecessary anxiety at bay for several years and counting. The reason is simple: she had finally mastered it.

If you put in the effort to learn how to walk, swim, bike, or drive, you'll never forget it. You have mastered it. It became part of your skillset. If you diligently learn how to master anxiety, you'll never forget it. Anxiety will never be able to dominate you *ever* again. It is well worth the effort!

I, for instance, can never go back to the anxious guy I used to be. I cannot unlearn what I have mastered.

I'm telling you Claire's story because you too will have setbacks. It won't be easy, and that's OK. You can keep referring to this book whenever you need it. If you've signed up to my mailing list on www.ilovepanicattacks.com, I'll keep sending you interesting techniques and videos every now and then as well.

You're not in this alone! You've got what you need now. Nobody can do it for you, but you won't need to reinvent the wheel. The techniques are there. Now it's up to you to test them until you master them. Remember, the power is already within you!

Conclusion

You've made it to the end of the main part of the book! The addendum that follows will go over some specific fears and symptoms.

Although this probably is only the beginning of your recovery, I want to congratulate you. So many people start reading self-help books and then stop after a couple of chapters when the going gets tough. You didn't.

I sincerely hope you will try the techniques and exercises I've been explaining throughout the book. They have the power to tame your anxiety.

Good luck with your journey in life. It was an honor to have you read this book. You could have done a thousand other things with your time, and you wisely chose to invest it in reading this book. I'm grateful for that. Even though I don't know you personally, I wrote this book with you in mind. That's where I got my motivation to keep writing during the many years I've been working on this book. I picture you trying the techniques and increasing the quality of your life.

So thank you!

And if you ever need more help than this book could offer, you know where to find me: www.ilovepanicattacks.com. There you'll find my free newsletter with a range of videos I've shot over the years and much more.

Good luck!

Warm regards,

Geert Verschaeve

Addendum: How to apply what you've learned on the most common sensations, symptoms, and situations that launch anxiety

Even though we've covered a variety of symptoms and situations throughout the book, let's go over the most common ones here and see what's going on and what you can do about it.

I want to re-emphasize that I am not a medical doctor. I will be speaking from personal experience, both from me overcoming my own panic attacks and anxiety, combined with all of the people I've been able to help, supplemented with scientific research here and there. If you suffer from any of the symptoms mentioned, even though you should never react with anxiety, you *should* have your health checked by a health care professional. Not to be reassured since that's a very short-term fix, but to be able to deal with any physical issue should there be one.

As I've explained, the goal is never to say, "Oh, it's probably nothing" and ignore it. The goal of what you're learning is to wipe unwanted anxiety off the table, regardless of whether something *is* going on or not.

Here's what I mean. I was in a fully packed auditorium in the center of London during a hot summer day last year. For some reason, there was no air conditioning, and the available oxygen was dropping swiftly. My body, sensitive as it is to a lack of oxygen, warned me by raising my heart rate and by giving me a slight shortness of breath. These were symptoms I was getting because of a real issue. I didn't ignore it, because something was going on. But I chose to say, "Thanks, kind canary in the coal mine. I know there's a lack of oxygen, but

I'm staying. Breathe and palpitate as you wish, I accept you." Symptoms were present; anxiety was not.

And within minutes, the feeling was gone. Because I didn't care. My body gave me a warning, one I didn't follow up upon, so it stopped warning me.

There is no way to completely avoid certain symptoms, and some circumstances may still give you a slightly heightened level of anxiety. That's normal and the goal of this book is not to avoid that. As I've explained, anxiety is necessary. It's just a warning. It would be impossible to not get warnings since your body still wants you to stay alive for as long as possible. The goal is to not be intolerant to those sensations, so we don't raise unwanted and unnecessary anxiety.

Please browse through the following pages. Skip what doesn't apply to you, and read what does. You'll find some additional insights and help.

Without a doubt, the most common consequence of being prone to anxiety is:

Having crazy thoughts and believing them

You wouldn't believe the types of thoughts my mind has come up with. Well, maybe you would, because I'm sure yours has generated some crazy thoughts as well.

Thoughts that would have made me break the law had I executed them. Thoughts that would have gotten me killed had I acted upon them. Thoughts that could have made me a millionaire or, on the contrary, bankrupt. I've had them all, just as you have.

Our thought machine never takes a break, not even when we're sleeping. That's when subconscious thoughts take over.

This thought machine is a powerful ally; yet, for people who suffer from anxiety, it becomes an enemy. Something they want to shut off and eliminate.

Look, we can't ask our thought machine to *just* come up with positive and constructive concepts. It cannot. It will come up with just about anything, from the most ridiculous to the most intelligent ideas anyone you know has ever had. And it's up to us to select what we need and discard what we don't.

Some of the thoughts will make you believe you're losing your mind; others will scare you because they will seemingly give you intentions you don't want to have.

It doesn't matter. They are just thoughts. Please let this sink in. They are just thoughts!

You don't have to agree with those thoughts, but you'll need to see them for what they are. Pieces of information.

You are not your thoughts. Having strange ideas doesn't make you weird or a bad person. This is not your *will*; these are not instructions that you will blindly follow. You are still in control.

You may be thinking, "Sure, Geert. But I have *so many* of these thoughts that I *must* be losing my mind." Well, please try to not think of a zebra now. Please do not think about a striped zebra running around in the sunshine eating some grass.

Impossible.

The more you resist, the more you will think about it. The stronger you react to certain thoughts, the more persistent they will be.

And that's the point. You are not your thoughts!

You are the thoughts you act upon. And you will not act upon thoughts that are not in line with your core.

If you are worried about your thoughts, this is proof that they are not who you are. Your crazy thoughts do not define you. It's like going across the channels on TV and passing by a horror movie with images you don't like. You react and zap to another channel. Then a news program you think is utterly boring, which you react to, and you keep zapping until you find something you like.

The same is going on with your thoughts. They are just channels of information; they are not you until you decide you like a certain channel and believe it sounds interesting. Only then do they become you.

And crazy thoughts are not just about losing your mind, going crazy, or doing something that you really wouldn't want to. They're also the famous "what if?" thoughts we've been discussing all throughout the book.

As always, even with the thoughts, full acceptance is key. Accept the stream of information you're getting, from the worst horror thoughts to the genius insights.

"Whatever! Thanks, mind, for your creativity, but I'm busy now. Unless you've got some real snakes, tigers, or aliens I need to look out for, I'm just going to continue with whatever I was doing prior to you disturbing me."

Imagine that you're sitting in a restaurant, enjoying your meal, and a kid walks by. That kid turns to you and says, "What if I start to freak out here? What if I faint? What if I vomit? What if I say something stupid?"

What will your reaction be?

"My gosh, yeah, what if?"

Probably not. Since it's not your kid, you may not even react at all and just turn back to your plate and continue eating. It's just a kid, and kids say the weirdest things.

Well, so does our crazy thought machine. And we can dismiss it just as easily as we can dismiss whatever a kid would say. Granted, it's a tiny bit harder because at first it doesn't seem to come from a distinct person, considering it's coming from within you. But look at your thought machine as that primitive kid who just blurts out whatever comes to mind.

If you suffer from bad panic attacks, your thoughts may try to make you believe that you will lose control. You will not. Your mind is simply overwhelmed because it is fighting against an imaginary army of ever increasing legions of tigers and other predators. You can't blame it for thinking *that* is a daunting task.

Nonetheless, here too, reassuring you that all will eventually be fine is not a solution, for your mind *will* try to convince you that your situation is different anyway. You know the rule by now: accept every possible outcome.

"Well, even if I lose my mind, even if I make the biggest fool out of myself, bring it on! It's about time. Whatever happens, it's OK." This cuts through everything.

Aside from our thoughts, symptoms can be troublesome as well. Without a doubt, the most common symptom is:

Heart palpitations, skipped heartbeats, and other weirdness related to the chest area

This is the number one response to adrenaline. It's difficult to have anxiety and not have it affect your heart. I had a tendency to place my finger on the vein in my neck, just to measure the status of my heart. If my heart was doing anything other than beating slowly, I'd panic even more and start the vicious cycle discussed in the beginning of this book.

We cannot really control our heart. Sure, our thoughts can help it calm down or speed up a bit, but if there ever would be a serious problem with our heart, our thoughts wouldn't be able to fix it.

The heart has many reasons to beat faster other than you being physically active. If you drink alcohol, your heart will beat faster since alcohol is a poison to our bodies. If you're sick and your immune system is fending off a virus, your heart will beat (a lot) faster. If you've eaten an ingredient you're allergic to, your heart will beat faster too. Nothing bad is going on then, your body is simply doing its job.

Irregular heartbeats are no source of concern either, provided your doctor confirmed you are healthy heart-wise.

Since overcoming my panic attacks, my approach truly has always been to just let my heart do what it wanted. For fourteen years, I thought I was going to die right then and there at least once per week. I now decide I prefer to die once, for real, instead of in my own imagination multiple times a week. I want to truly *live* in the mean time.

Good ways to deal with heart symptoms are to just accept them, to say, "Whatever happens, it's OK. If it's something bad, I'll deal with it then but now I'm still standing." Use the friend method and comfort yourself. Or push harder and say, "Is that all you've got? Beat faster!" Reconfirm that you're sick of being scared. You can also finally embrace it, letting the feeling of fear wash over you. Feel it, instead of frantically pushing it away like you probably used to.

Pick anything you like or a combo of everything, combined with the other techniques you've gotten on the menu in part two. Your heart is always going to mind its own business. We better let it.

This is indeed mostly a trust issue. Anxiety will only rise when you don't trust your heart to do the right thing. That's what the "what if?" thoughts will try to tell you. If they don't, your negative radio will most probably be adding, "Yeah but you know you're probably having a heart attack." To which my reply has become, "Whatever. Whatever happens it's OK, *even that.*" This was just my way of making fun of it and of accepting the anxiety. I, of course, preferred not to die!

I've been explaining how to use this sentence for over a decade to the people who followed the audio course, and the results have been nothing less than amazing. So give this a try, as hard and ridiculous as it may sound at first. I, personally, only worry if my heart doesn't beat at all. And that has so far never happened.

And as I said earlier, if the pain and symptoms are severe, you go to the emergency room or call for an ambulance, but you can still choose to do so without anxiety. As you've learned in part one, anxiety can give you all of the symptoms that may resemble heart problems, so the only way to know something may really be going on is when you choose to let go of the anxiety. If the symptoms and pain then persist, only then would I, personally, seek help. Anxiety has no place here, no role. It won't help even *if* something is going on. So it's totally safe to choose to let go of anxiety.

Red face, flushing, and sweating

This is a great one if you suffer from a social phobia. There you are, minding your own business while sitting or standing in a public setting, possibly in conversation with someone else and suddenly you feel the wave of warmth entering your face. You know what that means... your skin will start to look red in no time, *that* or sweat beads will start to form, mimicking the Niagara waterfalls on your forehead. And if they don't start on your face, they may do so in your arm pits before going for a collective run down your shirt.

A red face, flushing, and sweating are very common and normal during slight to moderate anxiety. A true panic attack, however, will probably give you a pale face, given that your blood will mostly rush to your muscles then. During moments of regular anxiety, however, the blood will rise to your head because that's where our brain tends to be. It needs oxygen and blood to operate well and find a way out of the possible predicament your amygdala believes you to be in.

Here too, pure acceptance is key. You can use any of the techniques mentioned in part two.

I like humor as a technique, with sentences like, "Other people have to pay to go to a sauna. I have one built in." And when someone notices your red face and comments on it, instead of feeling ashamed, state, "Yeah, well, you know how chameleons can change color? I've been practicing and practicing, but for now it only works with the red tone."

This form of anxiety can only hurt you socially when you let it, when you consider it as a weakness. It isn't. It's just a symptom. When you're hot, you sweat and get a red face. And sure, other people may not be feeling hot, but you are.

I want to emphasize this. Other people will see it, just like they can see you blink or wheeze, but they will not think any of the bad things your mind comes up with. They'll believe you're hot (which, to some, is a compliment) or possibly nervous. Is that so bad?

Let's imagine they think, "Djeezs, look at her. What a loser, she is *so* weak a falling rain drop would crush her." Does this say anything about you? Does it really? What does it say about the person thinking it? Who's the real loser here? It's not our job to adapt and dance to the whims of fools, crazy people, nasty people, bad people, stupid people, unkind people, and others. Let them have their opinion!

I still have sweaty armpits easily, not linked to anxiety. I don't hide them. I choose not to care. There are so many flaws and disadvantages to my body and me being me, just as there are some to you being you. Nobody is perfect. I've learned to love myself, flaws included.

The more you resist sweating or flushing, the higher the tension will be. When it is, you will flush and sweat even more. As soon as you feel it coming on, let it come. Say, "Whatever happens, it's OK. Make me as red as a tomato or a boiled lobster, it's OK."

Light-headedness and vertigo

This was one of the more prominent sensations I personally had to deal with.

Ingredients play a major role. Nobody acts surprised when they feel dizzy after downing a glass or three of their favorite liquor, but when I tell them the new furniture they bought may be causing it, they tend to look at me like I come from a different planet. Yet, the wood that's used in most furniture often off gasses a lot of harmful toxins like formaldehyde (chloroform).

When you suffer from these symptoms, as with every other symptom, talk to your doctor first. When your health seems OK, try to find what your body may be reacting to. It can be odors, ingredients, and substances you apply onto your skin. Fluoride in some tooth pastes causes vertigo for me, as do all artificial sweeteners. Start a diary and whenever you feel these sensations, write down where you were the twelve to twenty-four hours prior to the sensation. What had you been doing? What had you been drinking, eating, smelling, and applying onto your skin? Be as detailed as possible. The cause, the ingredient your body is responding to, is probably on the list.

Many years ago, I got severe vertigo with my vision going black. I had no idea what brought up the sensation, but I wrote everything down in my journal. Two months later, the same thing happened, and I wrote it down again. I noticed that I had just drank a freshly juiced apple juice, both times. So I started to do some research and found out that the pits of apples, which I hadn't removed prior to juicing them, contain cyanide, the powerful neurotoxin. My juicer had kindly juiced those pits as well, giving me apple juice with just a hint of cyanide. There you had it, I had found the cause.

On a mental level, apply any or all of the techniques learned in part two. I personally loved the statement, "Oh well, I'm going to let my body space out. I'll float with it and go with the flow." Don't fight it since additional stress will only make it worse. Pure acceptance, as always, is key.

Nausea and other digestive problems

These can be very disturbing since few people can ignore nausea. Nausea can be caused by ingredients, food intolerances, food allergies, spoiled food, viruses, pregnancy, motion sickness, and a whole range of other causes.

Always figure out what you ate, drank, applied to your skin, and even smelled in the twenty-four hours prior to the nausea. A chemical smell you inhale today (exhaust fumes or the smell of a new printer, for instance) can give nausea tomorrow.

Chances are, however, that nausea will come and bother you in social settings, when it's the last thing on earth you need.

At the risk of repeating everything like a parrot, you can best deal with it with by stating, "Oh well, I give myself to whatever happens now. It's all OK. Dear stomach, you can do what you believe is the right thing to do."

This is important for your stomach as well, because the more tense you are, the more your stomach will resist digesting whatever it should digest. Stress, anxiety, and bouts of panic *are causes* of nausea and not just the result.

If you ever meet a real tiger, your body will stop the digestion instantly so all of your energy can go to freaking out and running away. If, however, you freak out about the nausea itself, your body will stop your digestion for the same reasons, making it worse.

I loved the exaggeration technique here. I already mentioned it, but when I was in the movie theaters and I got nauseous, instead of running or at the very least ruining my movie experience, I thought, "Oh well, if I projectile vomit onto the screen and the ten rows of people in front of me, at least they'll have something tasty to dip their nachos into. That'll teach them for making all those crunchy noises. I'm ready, bring it on! Whatever happens, it's OK."

This was all I needed to calm down. If I had eaten something prior that was causing the nausea, the symptom itself persisted, but all of the negative emotions and anxiety that surrounded it subsided quickly. And more often than not it wasn't even because of what I had eaten, and my body and entire digestive system would start to relax again.

You can of course pick any of the other techniques from part two as well. They have worked very well for my clients who suffered from nausea or fear of vomiting.

Full acceptance is key. At first I used to run for the bathroom or at least make sure I'd know where the restrooms were so I could immediately get to them when needed. That's an avoidance strategy. It's still feeding the fear. It's still a contingency plan. And these just maintain the anxiety. It's time to go for a new approach, the one I've been preaching all throughout this book.

Shortness of breath

Hyperventilation is very common with panic attacks and anxiety. Here it will be important to forgo of the common technique of breathing in a bag since that will mess up your blood oxygen/carbon dioxide levels even more.

There are two ways to respond:

1. Do nothing and let your body breathe any way it wants. This is often the most effective approach. Our breathing happens automatically, and your body will soon find the best way of breathing.

2. Use abdominal breathing. Breathe in through the nose and out through the mouth, making sure that only your abdomen moves.

Furthermore, you can use any of the mental and other techniques described in part two of this book. My favorite is,

"I allow you to breathe anyway you like, dear body. Whatever happens, I'm fine with it!"

Oppressive feelings

I've discussed this very issue elsewhere in the book as well, but oppressive feelings will come from a built-in alarm that you have in your body. It will probably be warning you that you need to get out of wherever you are in at that moment (a plane, a meeting room, even something as big as a football arena).

I'll never forget the last time I had these feelings (after I had already overcome my panic attacks). I walked into a large stadium on a hot summer day, and it was packed with people. There was no roof on the stadium so both the sun and fresh air could get in. We had our own seats, but as soon as I sat down, I got that oppressive feeling and some vertigo and light-headedness.

I no longer panicked, but I couldn't help but notice the sensation. My body was warning me and asking me to get out of there. Then it hit me. There were plenty of people around me breathing in the oxygen and breathing out carbon dioxide. The stadium was roofless, but it was a warm summer day when the air isn't optimal anyway. My body has a very sensitive radar for this and told me right away. This alarm can save your life. I'm glad mine is sensitive.

You hear it often during the winter months in colder areas of the country: people die because of a carbon monoxide poisoning because they put on a stove or a fire place and have no adequate fresh air coming in. Their bodies didn't tell them the room was running out of oxygen.

That's what your body is trying to warn you for when you have feelings of oppression. It's saying there are too many people, not enough air, not enough space, GET OUT! It may even be triggering on something else too, but the conclusion stays the same: get out!

Nevertheless, as always, we don't *have* to listen. It's just a warning, and we get to decide how we respond.

Back to my stadium example. In the past, I would have panicked for about twenty minutes and then I would have probably left the stadium. This time, however, I simply told my alarm system, "Thanks, got it, but I'm safe here. There's no need to run." Within ten minutes, the feeling was gone. Yet, the people and the quality of the air remained the same. I didn't change anything. I simply dismissed the alarm.

Have you ever set foot in a bathtub with the water just a bit too hot, but you got in anyway? What happened? It probably burned for a while at first, your nerves were screaming, "CAUTION! This is hot. This is potentially dangerous. Don't even think about getting in" and then your body adapted and stopped warning you, figuring you had gotten the message.

The same happens when you get the feeling of oppression. It's just a warning, and then it's up to us to decide how we handle it. When you dismiss it and don't leave, the warning eventually goes away.

Pain in the chest

For this symptom, I would apply what I've described in the heart palpitations paragraph. Pain in the chest can come from a variety of causes and should be checked by your doctor, but here still, anxiety is not needed. It serves no purpose.

If the pain is caused by your stomach that dislikes what you ate, a beginning ulcer, or your liver that has a challenging task ahead, anxiety is not going to fix any of that.

Since we eat/drink things that our body dislikes, since we catch viruses and more, pains are possible. I always go for full acceptance and when a symptom persists, I have it checked and try to figure out what's causing it.

Besides the symptoms, here are some of the more common locations and situations that give people anxiety.

Fear of driving

This is a very common fear for a variety of reasons. In my home country Belgium, people who have a fear of driving are scared of all of the lunatics driving around on the roads. If you ever drive on a Belgian highway close to Brussels, you'll see that a lot of drivers go well over the speed limit and seem to love driving bumper to bumper.

In France, most of my clients with a fear of driving are afraid they can't get off the highway when they want, because there are areas of hundreds of miles without an exit on well-fenced toll roads.

In the US, the many lanes on most highways give some people the creeps. And in every country, I encounter people with a fear of:

-   bridges
-   tunnels
-   driving too far away from home
-   stop lights
-   traffic jams
-   trucks and big rigs
-   speed
-   getting involved in an accident
-   causing an accident
-   losing control
-   losing their mind while at the wheel

Interestingly, I mostly see people past the age of 40 who have previously driven around without problems, fighting with this type of fear.

Their mind comes up with dangerous scenarios out of nowhere. Collisions, causing a collision, fainting, no longer trusting the fact that they can control the car at all times and more.

Do these people have proof that all of the bad things their mind games come up with can indeed happen? Sure, it happens *all* the time in movies like *Die Hard*, *The End of the World* and *Godzilla*. In real life, these accidents aren't so frequent.

And even if some of the scenarios they fear are realistic, these people are still causing the anxiety all on their own, considering they are not *in* that precarious situation they're vividly imagining.

I've met people who were involved in actual, major car crashes, who spent time in the hospital for weeks and now still drive, without anxiety.

So here too, there's more at play than the actual location or the activity of driving. It's the anxiety we are adding by believing and following our thoughts and the many what-if scenarios they will serve. That's the true cause.

Why would the mind do this?

It has to. Driving is unnatural. There you are, driving around at speeds you could never ever run at, getting sensations both visually and physically that your body doesn't recognize as natural. Because of this, your radar is put on high alert. It *is* dangerous.

That's why, when you learn to drive, driving feels scary. The fast movement that your body senses and the many visual stimuli (other cars for one) that you need to take into account are strange and impressive. For most people, however, the confidence they gain by not crashing and by seeing other people drive around too, conquers this fear. They gain trust, and the amygdala and other alarm systems relax.

For some, this trust never came, and they fail to ever feel at ease. For others, that confidence gradually declines as they age or quickly deteriorates after a traumatizing experience.

When it happens later in life, it's just because the radar that handles all of the visual stimuli is having a much harder time to process everything because our brains slow down a bit with age. The danger radar consequently becomes much more sensitive.

You may have noticed that older people drive slower; they just need more time to process everything that happens at certain speeds.

This, of course, is not a reason to avoid driving. If you feel that your danger radar becomes more alert, thank it, and use any of the techniques discussed in part two to soothe yourself. There is no increased danger.

Life simply *is* dangerous. You are able to accept this perfectly well in most areas of your life, and it should be accepted while driving as well. Especially so because you are a good driver. Your alertness and danger radar make you a *better* driver!

Who are the ones causing the most accidents? Drunk people. People on their phones. That's because their alertness and danger radar is at sub-zero levels at that time.

Please remember this insight and repeat it to yourself should you start to see driving as dangerous. It's just your danger radar, and that's exactly the one that's keeping you safe. Compliment it, accept it, and let go.

For some people, the fear is different. They fear not being able to get out, losing their minds and causing an accident themselves, getting and staying stuck and so on. What I'm about to explain now works well on the previously mentioned driving fears and especially well here in what's to come.

Let go.

"Whatever happens, it's OK. I give up, I embrace, I accept, so be it!"

I won't repeat everything I explained in part two, but remember that even though some of the possible outcomes would not be OK, accepting them and ridiculously thinking they are fine is always better than ridiculously thinking there's a high probability the bad thing is going to happen. **Always choose the path of no anxiety.** You're fine, you're always fine, you always have been fine. And even when something bad happens, as the great Victor Frankl would say, you can choose to be fine.

The jolt of adrenaline and the weird sensations can be a bit harder to deal with while driving, because your body wants to run and move, and yet you're sitting strapped in in your unmovable car seat.

What works well here is to start singing loudly or yelling YIHA to use up some of the adrenaline. It's just excitement because you're doing something that your body considers exciting.

And let's face it, it *is*. Can you imagine how a cavewoman or caveman would have responded had we put them in the back seat of a car doing just thirty miles an hour? They would have been in shock and awe.

As you practice dealing with your fear of driving, you can take baby steps. You can go for practice runs at a quiet moment or jump into the deep end of the pool and drive in the middle of rush hour traffic. It's up to you.

Also know that it's totally fine if you have to stop and park the car to take a minute to calm down. Everything is OK, no matter how you choose to deal with it.

You can also install my app on your phone (you'll find a link on geertbook.com) and listen to the first session of my audio course (for free) while driving. If you need more, you can opt for the full course that you can find on my website. I once stopped next to a car at a traffic light and heard that the woman next to me was listening to my audio course. She was quite surprised to see me next to her when I said, "I know that voice" with a huge grin on my face.

When you practice, be proud! If you made it ten yards or ten miles, it doesn't matter.

And I mean that. If you suffer from a fear of driving, it's important to make it less important, to make it matter less. Just do it, go with the flow, and accept what you will feel. The more you can do that, the sooner the fear will start to subside.

Fear of flying

This is one of my favorites. Getting into an airplane with over a hundred people and not being able to get out for hours. That *and* who knows what happens when someone forgot to securely attach the wings to the plane...

You wouldn't believe the kinds of disaster scenarios my mind came up with while flying. I'm sorry, of course you would, you're probably experiencing many of those very same mind games as well.

With a fear of flying many danger radars will sound the alarm. First, there's a change in the oxygen levels on board as soon as the doors close. We're no longer breathing in pure, natural air, and the body senses it. For some people, me included, this will sound an alarm. It's the "get out of the coal mine" alarm that can launch a pounding heart, shortness of breath, nausea, possibly some vertigo, and a general feeling of malaise and discomfort.

This alone can be enough to act as a first trigger and launch the vicious panic cycle I discussed in the beginning. Don't let it, and just explain to yourself what's happening and why. It's just your body trying to warn you that you may need to pay attention and that something dangerous may be going on. When it does, it's always up to us to decide whether it is or not. And in this case, we all know flying is one of the safest ways to travel *and* that you're not going to fall without oxygen.

Then, there's the social aspect of the anxiety for some. All of my social fears arose here too, with the "what if I throw up, what if I lose my mind, what if I don't have an aisle seat and I want to get up?" thought train. For these specific fears, you can use what I'll explain in the next chapter about social fears.

The best way to deal with any of the fears you may have during flying is to sit back and relax... and *really* enjoy the flight like you are probably being told to.

It's been more than a decade ago since I was practicing my own fear of flying, but here's exactly what I told myself after I boarded a plane only to hear that I had been reassigned to a claustrophobic non-aisle seat that I had booked weeks in advance, just to be sure, of course:

"Look, Geert, I'm sitting down now, and I'm going to stay strapped in. I accept all of these weird sensations that I prefer not to feel. I'm going to accept all of the strange sounds the plane will make. I *give* myself to all of that. I'm going with the flow, I'm floating in the air, I'm letting it all flow over me, and I will not resist. *Whatever* happens, I'm game. It's all OK."

And as I was saying that, I emotionally let go of control. I gave my life to the pilots of the plane and was fine with everything. Yes, that sounds crazy, I know... and I hadn't even begun drinking a margarita like the lady next to me. No, not me, I wasn't going to drink my anxiety down, I wasn't going to push it away, I was ready to run toward it and give it the best cuddle it had ever had.

I had walked on board with serious bouts of anxiety, nearly erupting into panic attacks, but as I was using this kind of self-dialogue, I started to calm down.

I've never had a fear of flying since.

And I'm giving you my exact thoughts since I know literally what I told myself, but please know that I've gotten hundreds of testimonials of people who have followed my audio course over the years who managed to do the exact same thing, often using a different set of thoughts that worked just fine for them. You'll need to come up with your own soothing cocktail of words, using any of the techniques you've learned in part two of the book.

Here too, you can start small with a short-distance flight or go big and travel to the other side of the world like I personally did. It doesn't matter. If you suffer from a fear of flying, your first flight will be pure torture. Your mind will anticipate the flight weeks in advance. When it does, congratulate your danger radar for being there for you. And keep repeating like a broken record, "Thanks. I'll see it when it happens. I'll see it then, when the moment is there. I'll stop planning now. I'll see it on the very day of the flight."

The day of the flight, your anxiety system will do everything it can to stop you from boarding. Why wouldn't it? You've been reacting as if you're about to be stuck in a confined space with two hundred bloodthirsty tigers fighting for the overhead luggage compartments. Here too, keep congratulating your anxiety system but firmly repeat, "Dear anxiety, I'll take you with me. I love you as much as you love me. I'm even starting to love panic attacks, thanks to that weirdo I read that book from, so I'll just take you with me since you seem to want to join me." And then move ahead, *with* your anxiety.

Don't expect your anxiety to subside yet. Expect it to be there, allow it to be there, and move forward regardless.

Do not drink alcohol on or before the flight. This will make it much harder to use your positive self-dialogue and may increase your anxiety.

As you're in flight, not avoiding the anxiety is key. It's pointless to look at your watch and calculate how long you'll still have to put up with this, for if you do, you're only feeding the anxiety. We're not there to wait for the flight to end or the anxiety to subside (not even *that*); we're there to learn how to become friends with all of those dreadful feelings and thoughts. Learning to give in, to accept, and to go with the flow is key.

Try thinking, "I'm going to stay here for as long as you stay, dear anxiety, even after we've landed and I have arrived at my destination, I'll stay put. I'm here to learn to deal with you. I no longer run. I accept you. And if you don't like that, it's up to *you* to leave. I won't. I'll stay put for the return flight if needed."

I probably don't have to keep explaining why it's totally OK and even the goal to have these types of silly dialogues with ourselves. All of the anxious "what if?" thoughts are at the very least *as* silly and ridiculous.

And then you keep doing this as long as it takes. You can of course add anything from the menu you found in part two of this book. Any of those techniques works great against the mind games you'll get on board of a plane.

Fear in social settings

This is a very common fear for obvious reasons. It's tough to live your life isolated on a deserted island. There are a lot of other people out there if you don't want to live in total isolation, so whatever you do, there will be social settings you have to be a part of.

Even when I was a full agoraphobic, afraid to leave my own house, I still had to join the rest of my family every now and then during important occasions. I still had to go to school and later to work.

Many fears can come together in this area of socially tinted anxiety and panic attacks. You may fear certain symptoms and are scared to get them in front of others. You may fear making a fool of yourself. You may fear others will dislike you, dismiss you, reject you, or think you are weak/silly/stupid/not up to the task.

"Other people see me as a very strong woman" is what many women who secretly suffer from severe panic attacks tell me. And it's not an accident, they want to be seen as a strong woman; they are ashamed of the strange thoughts and sensations they are struggling with. Men, of course, suffer equally.

Embarrassment is indeed key, and most people with a social fear go to great lengths to avoid that embarrassment. This is *the* key in fact.

Here's what I mean. When you're sitting at a table in a restaurant and you get your dreaded symptom (for me that would have been nausea), it is not the symptom that scares you. *That's* not what you are afraid of.

Am I right?

Let me rephrase the question. Would you still fear your symptom if you were be walking around, alone, on a deserted island when it struck? Probably not. At least not so much.

The projected embarrassment is the cause of the fear. The feelings of shame and rejection are the originators.

This is a double-edged sword since on top of the preemptive embarrassment, you'll also feel trapped. On one hand, you have the symptom and sensations; on the other hand, you have the other people.

"One or both must go! Either the symptoms stop *or* I will have to move away from these people," your mind will conclude. And since you can't make the other people vanish, that gives your anxious mind a couple of options:

- excusing yourself, which is not always possible

- trying to manage your symptoms, which will probably make it worse thanks to the vicious cycle

So what are you to do? I'm sure you know the answer by now: <u>full acceptance</u>. "Whatever happens, it's OK. Bring it on; show me the worst you've got. I'm ready."

There is no other way. Worrying about or trying to suppress the symptoms will only feed them, will launch the vicious cycle, and make everything worse.

Avoidance or running away will temporarily decrease the anxiety, but your life will become a string of moments with anticipatory anxiety. Subsequently the dreadful social moment will come and pass, only to be followed by the anticipation of the next event on the calendar.

Full acceptance is key, but there luckily are some stepping-stones that can help you get there.

First, the sensation of being stuck is fake. It is created by your own mind. Here too, we'll have to think back of what Victor Frankl said, "Between stimulus and response, there is a space. In that space is our power to choose our response. In our response lies our growth and our freedom."

The stimulus is the symptom and the fact that other people are near, the response is whatever you choose it to be. This is a freedom nobody can take away from you. You can choose to respond with even more anxiety, as I diligently did during fourteen years, or you can choose any of the techniques from part two of this book.

When I got a panic attack in the movie theaters, it was because I thought I couldn't leave. I knew I could... but then other people would have to get up, my friends would ask me what happened, I would miss parts of the movie... so I was trapped. It was a major lose-lose situation.

When I had trouble during meetings or in restaurants, I knew other people would wonder why I had to urgently leave. They would question me about it afterward, my food would get cold, I would have missed important parts of the meeting, I would feel like a loser... so I thought I couldn't leave. Same goes for family get-togethers, shopping for groceries, and any of the other social situations.

First, we're not stuck. We can at the very least move around, *even* in an airplane, train, or an elevator. The feeling of being stuck is a mind game.

But it doesn't matter. There's no need to move or to leave!

You're fine where you are.

Please put that sentence on your bathroom mirror: "I'm fine wherever I am." The fear is fake; it's unwanted anxiety. You're not about to get eaten here either. There is no need to run because if you do, you're proving that *this* situation is indeed to be avoided, making it harder for the next time you're in the same or even in similar circumstances. That's the reason why my anxiety spread out like a wild flame in a batch of hay. From a family get-together where I had my first attack to restaurants, movie theaters, public transportation, and so on.

There's no need to run since the other location you're running toward isn't safer than where you were. Both are not dangerous. It's a perceived danger, not a real one (if it were, it would be real, wanted anxiety and running would actually be advised).

Now your mind may say, "Thanks, Geert, next time I'll force myself to stay." There's no need for that either.

Whatever happens, it's OK. You can leave, you can stay, it doesn't matter. Try to take away that pressure that you're otherwise adding onto your already sensitive nervous system. It's all OK.

What I did is I told myself: "I *can* leave, but I choose to stay. I want to sit this one out; I want to see what happens. I'm going with the flow; I allow all of my symptoms and sensations. I let it happen. I'm sick of running, I'm sick of worrying. It's time to see what happens when I stay."

Well... here too I came home empty handed. Nothing happened. Absolutely nothing. My symptoms stayed for about twenty minutes, the average time of every panic attack, and then they left. The tigers, sharks, utter and total humiliation, rejection, the end of my days, the end of everything... none of that came!

Let me tell you a great story of something that happened shortly after I had overcome my panic attacks. Here I was, out and about, living my life again. I'm out with a good friend and we're sitting in a very fancy restaurant. Very fancy. The kind where you don't want to cause any problems.

We had just ordered our dinner, and I was sipping from my mojito as my phone started to vibrate. I saw a text message stating, "Geert, I'm afraid I have bad news... " and then some news that was indeed really bad for me professionally.

It came as a shock and was totally unexpected. I had just defeated another major problem and thought I was going to be in the clear for a while. This dinner was meant as a celebration for overcoming that other issue, and the last thing I had expected that night was getting that text. Neither did my body and my all-time bestie: my amygdala.

Since I perceived that worrisome business news as danger, my amygdala was there to help and it tried to launch a major panic attack, thinking *that* would take care of it. Amazing. Only, not so much at that time.

Right away, I lost all visibility. It was pitch black in front of my eyes, and I could no longer see at all. Then I got a major wave of warmth through my body. The fact that I could no longer see my good friend, nor my mojito troubled me for a second.

But then I got it. I thought, "Wow, I just pushed the fire alarm. My amygdala thinks this bad news is going to kill me. Good job, little buddy. Although I'm not sure what losing my vision is meant for, but anyways, good job. The news is bad indeed and will have big consequences, but there are no tigers!"

No longer feeling ashamed I told my friend and even the waiter who came to check up on us: "I just got bad news and for some reason I can't see, but that's OK, my vision will come back" and I continued the conversation I was having with my friend. Exactly seven minutes later (my friend timed it), my vision slowly returned. I could think clearly again and the fog was gone.

The bad news was still there. Nothing had been fixed, but I had decided, "I can't change anything about it tonight. I received bad news, I got a bad stimulus, but I'm going to do what Victor Frankl said. I have the freedom to choose how I respond, and I'm responding by deciding that I will deal with it as of tomorrow. It's outside of my control for now anyway," and I had a great night.

This is indeed our last freedom, the one that nobody can ever take away. We do not decide what happens to us, but we always decide how we respond.

Allow your anxiety, don't resist, and then use any of the techniques from part two. Whatever the "what if?" that your mind comes up with, allow it, and say "Sure, whatever. I'll see it when it happens. Thanks for the warning."

On a final social note, I often get the question: "Geert, what do I do when fear hits me *during* a conversation. I then don't have time for a whole inner self-dialogue."

First of all, you do. During a conversation, your mind still goes into a thousand directions. Yet there is no need to spend time on panicking. For some people that image remains important, as in the other person shouldn't see that I'm feeling bad.

Shame is never good or needed. It takes courage to be open and authentic, so should you say, "I don't feel well, I think I'm having a panic attack... anyway, how are the kids?" then this takes proverbial balls. And other people know it!

Owning up to something and deliberately risking the embarrassment is much more courageous than frantically trying to hide what's happening. So should you feel the need, just explain what's going on.

Nevertheless, full acceptance is the solution here. No lengthy inner dialogue is needed when you don't have the time, just say, "Whatever, I give myself to what's about to happen and

I'll see it when it does" and continue the conversation. No resistance, no defense, just full acceptance.

This works miracles in every social situation.

And if you want more, here are some additional "I no longer care about what others think of me" exercises.

Expose yourself to them not liking you!

This is a tricky but important technique. The only way to master some activities is to actually do them. You cannot learn to ride a bike by reading a book or by watching a how-to YouTube video about it. You'll need to do it for real.

What if you could play around and push your limits by stepping outside of your comfort zone? I can tell you from firsthand experience that this is super liberating. Here's what I mean. If you're scared about what people think of you, chances are you're continuously adapting and making sure you don't step out of what's considered the norm. That is a continuous stress and pressure on your nervous system and will increase the likelihood of feeling anxiety, having a panic attack, and more.

The best way to step out of this is to see what happens when you risk people not liking you. Will it be as bad as you imagine?

That makes me remember one of my flights in the US about a decade ago. One guy was constantly cracking jokes. I don't know what vitamins he had taken prior to the flight but at one point he got up, looked around with a smile, and said, "Anyone want to join me and go for a smoke outside?"

Most people in his vicinity started to laugh. Some didn't care, and some probably wondered when he was going to be quiet. He, however, didn't care. He enjoyed himself and even got the phone number of the cute woman next to him. We all overheard that too.

So how do you go about testing this? Simply step out of your comfort zone, with that being the only goal.

When you're walking down a busy street, don't step aside for the people coming right at you. Take the risk of bumping into them. First of all, you'll see that most people will actually adjust their path and move out of your way. Second, when someone doesn't and you do bump into them, you can simply say "oops" and continue on. It's as much their fault as it is yours!

If you're a man, walk into the lingerie section of any major store and browse through the bras and hosiery. When someone asks if you need help say, "No thanks. I'm just browsing." This might feel really weird as if you're not supposed to be there. You'll have thoughts like "what will all of these people think of me?" That's exactly the point. The more you expose yourself to situations like this and actually survive them, the more your fears will melt away.

If you're a woman, go to the men's restrooms and pretend you don't care. When someone says something about it, you can say, "Thanks, I know" with a smile. And keep repeating that sentence if needed.

All of these examples will feel really awkward. Again, *that's* the goal! We need to learn to feel and accept unwanted emotions. That's how our comfort circle and especially our self-confidence grow.

A great one is to get into an already occupied elevator and instead of turning around and facing the door, keep facing forward, thus directly facing all of the people already in the elevator. Simply smile and then mind your own business.

As you can see, the goal is to put yourself *deliberately* in a socially awkward situation. If anyone gives you a negative remark during these exercises, simply smile. You will feel bad inside, but that too is the point. You're strengthening that muscle in order to get used to it.

The more you're in a socially awkward situation and you survive, the more your amygdala and brain will learn that there's nothing to fear. And since you've survived the *really* awkward moments, little things like giving a speech or having a romantic dinner will feel like walks in the park.

This exercise is a great way to enlarge your social comfort circle. Self-esteem comes from having the confidence that nothing bad will happen, that you know how to handle *it*. There's only one way to get there, and that's to practice.

Fear of getting trapped

If this is your fear, please go through the fear of flying chapter a couple of pages back. You can use everything I explained there when you fear:

- elevators
- the dentist's chair
- surgery
- medical scans

- getting stuck in a submarine stuck in enemy territory

It's the exact same alarm system that goes off while flying.

Needing a safe spot nearby

I won't spend too much time on this one since I've already discussed it earlier in the book. But many forms of anxiety, like a social phobia, agoraphobia, and even fears like a fear of driving come with needing a safe zone, a safe spot.

This will often be your own home, but it can be ad-interim homes where you can seclude yourself for a couple of minutes like the restrooms.

These are not needed. Unless it's wanted and real anxiety because of the real physical danger you're in, you're as safe wherever you are at the moment the anxiety strikes as you would be in your own home. Plus, as I've noticed during the years I had actual agoraphobia, the anxiety will simply find you wherever you try to hide anyway.

You cannot outrun it.

It's like the ghosts you see in the movies. While the protagonist tries to run, the ghost keeps reappearing and when the protagonist thinks he's safe after shutting a door, as soon as he turns around there is that ghost again.

Anxiety cannot be outrun, and we don't even need to, as explained. You are your safe spot. The world is your backyard. All the rest is trivial and just a mind game.

I always loved it when people who started the audio course told me, "Well, Geert, I feel perfectly fine, as long as I stay within a ten-mile radius from my home. Outside of that radius all hell breaks loose."

Right... because indeed, the danger is different at eleven miles than it is at a nine-mile distance from the home. Of course it isn't, but your mind wants you to believe so. These are just mind games.

As soon as these people drove outside of their radius, they had already tensed up their nervous system by thinking, "Oh my, I'm coming closer to the end of my comfort circle. I hope I survive it." Then as they got at the ten-mile distance they added, "Oh no, this is where the anxiety will start. I'm very far away from home now, and there are no hospitals around. I hope I survive this. What is this that I'm feeling there? Oh no!"... and the avalanche starts. They created it.

And I'm, of course, not pointing fingers here; my anxiety started not with the amount of miles but the amount of minutes. I always wanted to be a set amount of minutes away from safety.

I've had clients who were good at ruining every vacation for their entire family, because of this anxiety. As soon as they were too far away from home, they got off balance while the physical danger they were in was the exact same as at home. Their minds were doing the rest.

Here, firstly, it's important to deal with the anticipatory anxiety. People with this type of fear will be dreading the trip for as long in advance as they can. They will go over all of the possibilities and prepare better than the CIA would for a regular mission. Don't do it. Allow your mind to come up with any "what ifs" it wants but firmly keep repeating like a broken record, "I'll deal with it on the day it happens, NOT beforehand." You'll have to repeat this often, because your danger radar won't give up.

That's normal! Our bodies are still equipped with the defense systems we needed ten thousand years ago. At that time, going away from home *was* dangerous. You could get eaten by predators you had never seen before, get hunted down by a rival clan from another town you had never heard of, eat from unknown berries that turned out to be poisonous... the list goes on.

That's why your body still tries to prepare. It doesn't know we've moved ahead with our civilization since it takes thousands of years for our instincts and genes to fully change.

Everything that's outside of our comfort zone will give anyone some form of fear. Everyone. How we react to it is what makes the difference.

From now on, take the anxiety with you. Step out of the bounds of your comfort circle, that's where the magic happens. You can use any of the techniques from part two to help you.

This concludes the addendum.

This is the real end

I hope you've enjoyed the book and that it has given you a lot of "aha!" moments that will propel you forward.

I need your help, however. I am a one-man army, trying to help as many people as I can, and I hope you'll be spreading the word.

What you can do to help is simple: please leave a review of the book on Amazon. You simply go to your order history, find the book, and then leave a review (or just search for the book and hit the "write a review" button). If you didn't like the book for some reason, please reach out to me directly on geert@geertbook.com. I value your feedback, even if it's negative. If you loved reading it, please share it on Amazon.

This will help support other people who still suffer from unwanted anxiety and panic attacks. They could use your help. People who suffer from anxiety will feel less alone when reading your message, and hopefully they will, thanks to you, find the courage to do something about it like you just did.

Thanks for sticking with me till the very end! It was a privilege to write this book for you.

Good luck!

Geert
Ilovepanicattacks.com

CPSIA information can be obtained
at www.ICGtesting.com
Printed in the USA
LVHW031452240320
651049LV00010B/1478

9 789090 305264